JOSH HARRISON & TODD PROCTOR

EMPOWERED

*Pastoral Perspectives on Life
& Leadership in **the Spirit***

with contributions from **HARVEY CAREY,
KATHLEEN DOYLE, DARREN ROUANZOIN,
CRAIG SPRINGER, CHRIS WIENAND & JON TYSON**

≡XPONENTIAL⌐

Empowered: Pastoral Perspectives on Life and Leadership in the Spirit
Copyright © 2021 by Josh Harrison and Todd Proctor

Exponential is a growing movement of activists committed to the multiplication of healthy new churches. Exponential Resources spotlights actionable principles, ideas, and solutions for the accelerated multiplication of healthy, reproducing faith communities. For more information, visit exponential.org.

Alpha is a series of sessions exploring the Christian faith and is designed to create conversation in a comfortable setting. Alpha takes place all around the globe— whether in a cafe, a church, a university or around a kitchen table—and everyone is welcome. No two Alphas look the same, but they all have three things in common: food, a talk, and good conversation. You can learn more about Alpha at alphausa.org.

All rights reserved. No part of this book, including icons and images, may be reproduced in any manner without prior written permission from copyright holder, except where noted in the text and in the case of brief quotations embodied in critical articles and reviews.

Unless otherwise indicated, all Scripture quotations are taken from the Holy Bible, New International Version®, NIV®. Copyright © 1973, 1978, 1984, 2011 by Biblica, Inc.® Used by permission of Zondervan. All rights reserved worldwide. www.zondervan.com. The "NIV" and "New International Version" are trademarks registered in the United States Patent and Trademark Office by Biblica, Inc.®

Scripture quotations marked ESV are taken from the ESV® Bible (The Holy Bible, English Standard Version®). Copyright © 2001 by Crossway, a publishing ministry of Good News Publishers. Used by permission. All rights reserved.

Scripture quotations marked MSG are taken from The Message. Copyright © 1993, 2002, 2018 by Eugene H. Peterson. Used by permission of NavPress. All rights reserved. Represented by Tyndale House Publishers, a Division of Tyndale House Ministries.

All emphases in Scripture quotations have been added by the author.

ISBN: 978-1-6242406-3-8 - Print
ISBN: 978-1-62424-065-5 - eBook

Edited by Jan Greggo & Krysti Hall
Cover Design by Kaleb Tapp
Interior Design by Harrington Interactive Media (harringtoninteractive.com)

Printed in the United States of America

ΞXPONENTIAL⌐

RESOURCING CHURCH PLANTERS

- 90+ eBooks
- Largest annual church planting conference in the world (Exponential Global Event in Orlando)
- Regional Conferences - Boise, DC, Southern CA, Bay Area CA, Chicago, Houston and New York City
- Exponential Español (spoken in Spanish)
- 200+ Roundtables on Topics like Church Multiplication, Mobilization, Church Planting, Emotionally Healthy Leaders, The Future of the Church, and More
- Exponential HUB - Free Digital Platform offering content & conversation (multiplication.org/HUB)
- FREE Online Multiplication & Mobilization Assessments
- FREE Online Multiplication & Mobilization Courses
- Conference content available via Digital Access Pass (Training Videos)
- Weekly Newsletter
- 1000+ Hours of Free Audio Training
- 100s of Hours of Free Video Training
- Free Podcast Interviews

exponential.org

Twitter.com/churchplanting
Facebook.com/churchplanting
Instagram.com/church_planting

≡XPONENTIAL

MARCH 7-10, 2022
ORLANDO, FL

"You will receive power when the Holy Spirit comes on you."

Acts 1:8

≡MP🔥WERED

| CHRISTINE CAINE | MICHAEL CARRION | DAVE FERGUSON | PETE GREIG | SHODANKEH JOHNSON | DANIELLE STRICKLAND | ALBERT TATE | KELVIN WALKER |

$19 OFF
with code
EMPOWERED2022

JOIN US AS WE JOURNEY TOGETHER TOWARDS:

- AN EMPOWERED HEART
- AN EMPOWERED LIFE
- AN EMPOWERED CULTURE
- AN EMPOWERED MOVEMENT
- AN EMPOWERED MOMENT

2022 CONFERENCE HIGHLIGHTS:

5000+ Church Multiplication Leaders | 175+ Speakers | 40 Tracks
15+ Pre-Cons | 200 Workshops | Sunny Orlando, FL

Register now at:
exponential.org/2022

People today are looking for a space to process life's deepest questions.

You can create that space.
We can help.

Learn more at alphausa.org

INSIDE

THERE MUST BE MORE

Todd Proctor

. . . .

"Come, Holy Spirit."

One of the oldest prayers of the church, known in some traditions as the *epiclesis*, has never been more needed. In some of the earliest gatherings of Jesus' followers, these were the words welcoming God's presence into the broken bread of the Eucharist. Now in our time, this cry is being reclaimed to call God's presence to invade the brokenness of our world.

At the time of this writing, the world seems to be unraveling at almost every seam. A global pandemic has been unleashed. Longstanding racial injustices are being exposed. The political landscape of the US is marked by deep and hostile divides.

Like a fractured windshield, the cracks spread with each new headline. Fear looms that perhaps one more devastating newsflash could shatter life as we know it beyond repair.

These growing uncertainties, and the deep questions they carry, appear to set the stage perfectly for the collective church to "rise and shine." At least, that seems like the way the story should unfold.

The reality is most pastors are fighting to keep their heads above water. Many of those positioned to lead the church forward are crippled with discouragement and disorientation like never before. So much of what used to inspire and mobilize our communities seems fruitless in this moment through which we are being called to navigate ourselves and others. Attempts at quick fixes to buoy ourselves and those inside our churches fall short. We need more than we can bring on our best day with our best vision, staff, or sermon.

In a strange way, this is right where God wants us. It is in these moments of openhanded desperation that his best work truly begins.

As proclaimed by Scottish pastor Oswald Chambers over a century ago, "Complete weakness and dependence will always be the occasion for the Spirit of God to manifest His power."[1]

In other words, we were never intended to become our own provision or rescue in times of need. Instead, embracing our utter helplessness is often the most strategic move on the board.

This was the posture of King Jehoshaphat. When faced with not one but three armies converging to unleash their collective wrath on Israel, he responded with an unconventional confession of total dependence:

> We do not know what to do, but our eyes are on you.
> (2 Chronicles 20:12b)

His choice to lead through reliance on God's presence and provision paved the way for an unlikely yet decisive victory.

This crossroads is always before us as leaders. In truth, what seems more obvious in times of crisis is just as relevant in times of calm. Our dependence is *always* the occasion for his power. And for generations of men and women who have answered the call of leading the church into the future, this simple prayer has been a gift that keeps on giving . . .

"Come, Holy Spirit."

The first time I remember hearing this prayer in public—or any setting—was "across the pond" in London. I had recently and very unexpectedly assumed the lead pastor role of a young, growing, but suddenly broken church in Orange County, California. As the founding worship pastor, I felt infinitely more at home behind a keyboard than a pulpit. But when our four-year-old community was hit with a potentially devastating leadership collapse, I was invited, for at least the interim, to take the lead. And as he so often does, God invested my unqualified availability in ways that would end up bringing him undeniable glory.

As I was just getting my bearings, my crash course in leading through crisis landed me in the UK. A retired Vineyard pastor named Don had taken me under his wing, which quickly led to an invitation to an overseas meetup with some compelling new friends with cool accents. Don became my greatest mentor in ministry. And that trip became a game-changing exposure to a different way of living and leading.

I was a sponge in those days, desperate to learn anything that would help our church weather our storm and lay claim to a new future. And as I took the posture of watching and learning, I quickly noticed that corporate prayer seemed to play out much differently in British church culture.

My years of growing up in church had given me the perspective that prayer was mostly a one-way conversation. Simply put, one took a need—whether for yourself, a friend, a distant aunt, or impoverished country—and presented it to God through a heartfelt, eyes-closed request. That was about the sum of it, as any response to these prayers seemed pending till an undisclosed later time.

But what I experienced on that trip with Don was a clear expectation for God to actually, experientially move in the here and now. Repeatedly we found ourselves in meetings and moments, large and intimate, when space was created for God not only to hear but respond. This was always preceded by the simple, ancient, non-hyped invitation . . .

"Come, Holy Spirit."

What I had for decades of near-perfect church attendance understood to be a one-directional plea was revealed to be a multidimensional exchange. People were undeniably affected in these moments, whether simply encouraged, deeply moved, or overcome with emotion. Stories of clarity, courage, healing, and strengthening flowed from this space created through, for the most part, simply waiting. This wasn't just about releasing cries and cares to God. It was about chances to release control to him, and then receive needed, unexpected gifts from him.

This awakening was both disorienting and compelling. In some ways, I found myself feeling shortchanged. How, as a then thirtysomething, seasoned follower of Jesus who had sat in countless church gatherings and prayed countless prayers, had I missed the memo that God was ready and willing to go off the script of our well-crafted plans?

This trip sparked an insatiable curiosity to know what it meant, theologically and experientially, for God to move in moments. I didn't want to settle for less than everything he is and everything he wants to do—not just for my own sake, but for the sake of thousands I was now pastoring.

I quickly realized this had huge pastoral implications. Even as I was still learning the ropes of leading a church, the conviction that "there must be more" haunted me. How could, and should, this kind of Spirit-led dependence and expectancy shape the culture of our church? Our community was in a huge restart and rebuild already—a true Nehemiah moment. I longed for this newfound conviction to be more than another add-on, to somehow be sown into the very foundation of our future.

There was a huge learning curve ahead of us. Most of the churches in our immediate geographic proximity did not seem to be aimed in the same direction. And there was no lack of thriving churches in Orange County. In fact, one friend called our region the "Holy Coast," referring to how many large, successful communities coexisted there.

Yet it often seemed like the momentum of attendance and impact could be largely explained by human strengths and strategies. In this region, recognized as one of the nation's epicenters of consumer

culture, the combo of inspiring teaching, cool music, fun kids'
programs, comfy seats, and craft coffee was usually a winning hand.

My trip to London seeded a holy dissatisfaction in our
community that we couldn't shake. Even as the "right pieces" began
to be reassembled, they just weren't enough. Even as seats, and then
services, began to be added, they also fell short. There was a growing
longing among our core of leaders to experience more and more of
what could only be explained by God.

That's why I kept returning to London, often with other pastors,
to further my reeducation. These times were as much about "soaking"
as they were about learning. So many epiphanies that ended up
shaping our culture came from sitting, observing, waiting, and
receiving in unforced moments that were infused with supernatural
power and purpose. These moments were usually inaugurated with
the increasingly familiar prayer . . .

"Come, Holy Spirit."

This was clearly much more than doing liturgical diligence. It was
a "welcome mat" for God to do his work, his way, in his people. And
it gave language to the culture of invitational expectancy that had
been forged in this deeply post-Christian and post-church reality.

I came to realize that for at least a generation in the UK, the
question wasn't, "Where do you go to church?" but instead, *"Why
would you go to church?"* The historic Anglican tribe, which was
inextricably embedded into the political and cultural fabric of the
UK, had become largely irrelevant. Stunning, stained-glass cathedrals
across the country had emptied of people and potency. And for
decades, the hope of true, widescale renewal seemed a fading mirage.

My friend Jeremy Jennings served in leading the prayer efforts
of one church community through these desert years. Though
strategically positioned in the posh center of London, this church
was one of many that had been pared down to a faithful but aging
remnant. Through a series of unexpected events, a hunger for greater
empowerment of the Spirit began to capture the hearts of leaders

there. Holding consistent, passionately engaged prayer meetings with time and space to encounter God seemed to be one of the keys to raising the temperature of expectancy in their lives, gatherings, and ministries.

As confirmation of this conviction, Jeremy recounts reading a full-page article in one of the local papers that detailed declining church attendance and spiritual interest across the nation. The headline read, "The Church on Its Knees." But what the *Daily Telegraph* declared as the problem, Jeremy knew was actually the solution: the church, starting with their church, on its knees! This was the welcome mat of desperation needed as an ongoing invitation for the Spirit to come.

Vibrant, sustained prayer ministries became the lifeblood of this church that would ultimately be ignited in ways that would change the world. Holy Trinity Brompton has become a hub of awakening and renewal across England that continues to this day—raising up hundreds of new leaders, replanting dozens of communities, and pioneering the Alpha Course, which has helped millions across the world discover Jesus. The story there continues to be a sustained, united commitment to Spirit-led and empowered ministry.

This is just one of many examples of leaders and communities I have encountered in recent years that are embracing increased reliance on the work and power of the Spirit for whatever the future holds. In truth, this should be the DNA every church carries, as from this source spring the roots of our family tree. A quick reading of the opening chapters of Acts refamiliarizes us with the original story that a ragtag group of wide-eyed, open-handed, ill-equipped but faith-filled pioneers was taken way off script to write. Their part was humble, courageous availability. What happened in and through them could only make sense because they waited for, and ultimately received, a power source that was completely outside of themselves.

We are self-deceived if we think we need this—need him—any less. In the sobering words of New York pastor Jon Tyson (who authors a chapter of this book), "So much content in the church, so little power." As we swim in an endless flood of innovative options, so much of the church seems devoid of the presence and power that is supposed to set us apart. Like the latest evolution of the iPhone, a brilliant design and bigger capacity are nothing but a dead weight without a battery, without a power source.

This challenge was prophetically indicted by theologian A. W. Tozer decades ago:

> If the Holy Spirit was withdrawn from the church today, 95 percent of what we do would go on and no one would know the difference. If the Holy Spirit had been withdrawn from the New Testament church, 95 percent of what they did would stop, and everybody would know the difference.[2]

How much truer have these words become in our time? We need more than new messengers, models, or means. We need a fresh awakening, filling, and commissioning to lead with a power that is not our own. And we need pastors who will once more lay claim to the cry:

"Come, Holy Spirit."

Throughout this book, you will hear the stories and convictions of leaders who are deeply committed to the journey of discovering and embracing more of what can only be explained by the power and presence of God. My good friend Josh Harrison has done skillful work in laying out a biblical foundation in each chapter for how the Spirit fills and fuels our lives and communities in vital ways. Josh and I have partnered together for many years in both megachurch and house church contexts. He is a humble, brilliant, boots-on-the-ground pastor who is passionate about both anchored theology and expectant encounters.

As Josh takes the lead through each chapter in exploring this empowered call, you will then be introduced to other friends—

courageous planters and pioneers of churches across the nation—who will share ways these convictions have been worked out in their contexts. They don't offer aspirational theories. They document discovered wisdom that comes from being called beyond their comfort zones to lead others where they first ventured themselves. As you read their unique accounts, take note of the holy discontent they each carry. Each author has been personally and pastorally captured by a longing for more than they could preach, build, or imagine on their best day in their own efforts. I have witnessed firsthand the ways they have been irrevocably wrecked and recalibrated for a new way of empowered living and leading.

As we have all partnered together on this project, our collective hope is that these insights and stories will offer both needed encouragement and practical equipping for the leadership journey you are on. Confronted with more unknowns than most of us have ever faced, it is vital to remember that uncharted waters can also hold exhilarating adventure when we invite God to take the rudder and send the wind.

> Call to me and I will answer you and tell you great and unsearchable things you do not know. (Jeremiah 33:3)

Let's accept this invitation, and offer one of our own . . .
  "Come, Holy Spirit. Guide us, fill us, empower us to more."

FIRST THINGS FIRST

Josh Harrison

And hope does not put us to shame, because God's
love has been poured out into our hearts through
the Holy Spirit, who has been given to us.

— Romans 5:5

· ·

The power of the Holy Spirit is love.

This is where we must begin because the way we start this journey will shape its outcome. Our launch trajectory determines our destination, and when it comes to life with God—which is what we are talking about whenever we talk about the Holy Spirit—there are all sorts of ways we can head off in the wrong direction. We all carry with us notions of what we think God is like—some of which we are aware of, many we're not. These notions, acknowledged or not, affect our lives in profound ways. In his book, *The Knowledge of the Holy*, theologian A. W. Tozer writes:

> What comes into our minds when we think about God is the most important thing about us? . . . For this reason the gravest question before the Church is always God Himself, and the most portentous fact about any man is not what he at a given time may say or do, but what he in his deep heart conceives God to be like. We tend by a secret law of the soul to move toward our mental image of God. This is true not only of the individual Christian, but of the company of Christians that composes the Church.

Always the most revealing thing about the Church is her idea of God, just as her most significant message is what she says about Him or leaves unsaid, for her silence is often more eloquent than her speech.[3]

I'm inclined to take this idea a step further and say this is true not only of the church but also of every human being, regardless of religious affiliation. Our lives are all built on our relationship with the divine, even if we think we don't have any relationship with the divine. In fact, an atheist is just as impacted by their atheism as a devout Christian is by their Christianity, but that's another conversation for another day. The point here is simply we are about to embark on a journey into life in the Holy Spirit, and if we want to end up in a place (not that this journey has an end; we will never reach the end of the inexhaustible) that's worthy of who he is and what he wants to do in us and through us, it's vitally important we start our journey pointed in the right direction.

You likely picked up a book titled *Empowered* expecting to learn about and grow in power. And there's nothing wrong with that. In fact, if that's why you're here, you won't be disappointed. The Holy Spirit is indeed the Empowerer, and Jesus has promised that power to his disciples, many times over. Luke makes this especially clear:

The angel answered, "The Holy Spirit will come on you, and the power of the Most High will overshadow you. So the holy one to be born will be called the Son of God." (Luke 1:35)

Jesus returned to Galilee in the power of the Spirit, and news about him spread through the whole countryside. (Luke 4:14)

When Jesus had called the Twelve together, he gave them power and authority to drive out all demons and to cure diseases. (Luke 9:1)

I am going to send you what my Father has promised; but stay .
in the city until you have been clothed with power from on high.
(Luke 24:49)

But you will receive power when the Holy Spirit comes on you;
and you will be my witnesses in Jerusalem, and in all Judea and
Samaria, and to the ends of the earth. (Acts 1:8)

We ought to come to him with the expectation of power, but if we
learn anything from history (and current reality), it's that power for
power's sake is never a worthy pursuit. In fact, that's how things tend
to go very wrong. There is nothing inherently wrong with power. We
were created to be powerful, to have agency, even sovereignty, over
not only ourselves but also the world around us.

God blessed them and said to them, "Be fruitful and increase in
number; fill the earth and subdue it. Rule over the fish in the sea
and the birds in the sky and over every living creature that moves
on the ground." (Genesis 1:28)

We were made to reign in this place. Clearly, power itself is not the
problem. It is a gift given by God, a tool to be used in a specific
context for a specific purpose. But like every tool, it can be misused,
wielded in ways the Giver never wanted.

The same is true of the power of the Holy Spirit. If you've been
around the church for any extended length of time, you'll know
there are generally two types of churches when it comes to the Holy
Spirit: those that talk about him and those that don't. This is, of
course, a gross oversimplification, but I think you know what I'm
talking about.

There are churches that describe themselves as "Spirit-led" and
spend a great deal of their time in conversation about and pursuit
of the Holy Spirit. We typically call these churches Pentecostal or
charismatic. Then there are churches that rarely, if ever, talk about

the Holy Spirit, focusing instead on the other two members of
the Trinity.

I've spent a bunch of time in both types of churches, and I've
learned a couple of things along the way.

From my experience in charismatic churches, I've learned that
it's possible for people who genuinely desire to live life in and by the
power of the Holy Spirit to get it wrong sometimes. Not everything
that happens in these churches is the Holy Spirit, and sometimes,
even with the best of intentions, people get hurt by other people in
his name.

From my time in non-charismatic churches, I've learned there are
a lot of people who have been hurt by (or at the very least, weirded
out by) charismatic churches and therefore have a certain reticence
whenever he comes up. Often in these contexts, if the Holy Spirit
comes up at all, it happens during the benediction where God
is referred to as the "Father, Son, and Holy Ghost," which, quite
frankly, always weirded *me* out a bit.

The point here is that it is possible for the power of the Holy
Spirit to be misused and for people to be damaged in the process. But
we must never forget the classic axiom: the remedy for misuse is not
no use but right use. Jesus has graciously promised his followers the
power of the Holy Spirit, and he has delivered on that promise. If we
ignore or refuse that gift because we are worried about its misuse, we
will miss out on the full, abundant, springs-of-living-water-filling-
us-up-and-pouring-out-of-us life that Jesus offers, and the world will
miss out on a Church fully alive and empowered to be a part of God's
mission to redeem the world.

So how do we not miss out? How do we ensure we are rightly
using the power of the Holy Spirit? That's the question this book
will seek to answer. And rather than making you wait until the end,
here's the answer right up front: for the gift of the power of the Holy
Spirit to be used correctly, we must first understand the character of
the Giver.

- Who is he?
- Why has he given us this gracious gift?
- How does he expect us to use it?

These questions are essential as we approach this conversation about the Holy Spirit. And the answer to each of these questions is "love." God is love. He has given us his Holy Spirit because he loves us and loves the world. He intends for us to use the gift of the Holy Spirit to love him, love one another, and love the world.

If we were to survey the whole Bible, we would see the Holy Spirit in many different contexts doing many different things. Sometimes he guided His people to a spacious place. Sometimes he led them into exile. Sometimes he empowered them for battle (or fought the battles directly on their behalf) and delivered them from the hands of their oppressors. At other times he judged his people for their idolatry and oppression of others. Often, he inspired and empowered great leaders—priests, prophets, judges, and kings—to guide his people into his vision of vitality and purpose. He appeared to them in many different forms—as breath, wind, cloud, fire, water, and a dove, to name a few—and many different places from the wilderness to the promised land and everywhere in between. Sometimes his hand was heavy on them and his voice loud in their ears; other times they struggled to know if he was with them at all, his presence distant, his voice just a whisper.

When we are dealing with the God within whom this entire diverse universe exists, there is quite literally no end to his creative self-expression. He is, without question, the most interesting person in the world. Yet throughout all the diversity and creativity of the manifestation and work of the Holy Spirit, there is a consistent thread that runs unbroken from the beginning of the Bible to the end (and beyond): God is intimately involved in his creation through his Spirit and gives the gift of his Presence, his Spirit, to his people out of the abundance of his love for them and the world.

In the Gospel of John, Jesus said it like this:

> If you love me, keep my commands. And I will ask the Father, and he will give you another advocate to help you and be with you forever—the Spirit of truth. The world cannot accept him because it neither sees him nor knows him. But you know him, for he lives with you and will be in you. I will not leave you as orphans; I will come to you. (John 14:15–18)

There's been a lot of talk over the centuries about the word Jesus used here to describe the Holy Spirit, *parakletos*, and there should be. It is a powerful and beautiful word. In fact, we're going to talk quite a bit about it in just a moment. But before we dive into the Greek to understand better the depths of what Jesus was saying, let's not miss what's right on the surface in plain English.

Did you hear how Jesus, the person most qualified to teach us about the Holy Spirit, talked about the Spirit's coming? He described it as an adoption. "I will not leave you as orphans; I will come to you." Depending on your cultural background or family history, it's possible to miss the power of this statement.

For many of us, the word "adoption" carries negative connotations. As a child of the '80s, I remember a familiar sitcom trope that involved a teenager rifling through a stack of papers found hidden in a closet and discovering their own adoption papers. Inevitably, what followed would be a series of misadventures as the teen quickly devolved into a full-blown identity crisis, followed by a confrontation with well-intended but comically misguided parents, then a touching but shallow reconciliation, a remarkably simple synthesis of this newly discovered truth into the youth's identity, and, finally, a requisite joke to make us all feel good and keep us coming back for more.

I can't tell you how many times I saw this storyline as a child, and while it may have passed for good comedy in the '80s, it also taught a generation of people like me that adoption wasn't something to be talked about in polite society. If you, for whatever reason, adopted a child, you shouldn't talk about it and should pretend as if it had never happened because you wouldn't want the adopted child to feel "less than." There's the problem: somewhere along the way someone convinced us that adoption was a qualitatively lesser experience than having "our own kids." As a result, we have parents (in sitcoms and real life) hiding adoption from their kids, we have adopted kids feeling like they're not allowed to talk about it, and we have countless people who assume people only adopt when they're left no other choice.[4]

This was not the case in the first-century Roman Empire where Jesus spoke these words and where the readers of John's Gospel lived. They never would have read Jesus' statement, "I will not leave you as orphans," as some sort of second-best, less-than experience. You see, there are four things we need to know about Roman adoption to grasp fully the impact Jesus' words would have had on the disciples who heard them and the early readers who encountered them in the Gospel.

First, adoption in the Roman Empire was not necessarily reactive; in other words, it was not always a Plan B. In that context, adoptive parents were almost always wealthy people—often senators or other high-ranking officials—who initiated adoption processes for the sake of securing a male heir to their fortune and legacy. What's fascinating about this is they would often adopt *before* knowing whether they could have a biological son. We must understand we're talking about vast fortunes, limited life expectancy, and uncertain political and social environments. There was simply too much at stake to wait on the possibility that somewhere down the line you might have a biological son who would eventually inherit and carry on the family name. So wealthy people would often engage in adoption *as their Plan A.* It was their first choice, and any biological children would find themselves playing second fiddle to the adopted heir.

Second, because adoption was primarily entered into by wealthy people intent on securing a male heir, it was incredibly expensive. There were no orphanages or foster systems in the Roman Empire, and often the children who were being adopted by these rich families were not actually orphans. Many times, wealthy people would approach someone from a lesser family who had a son (usually their firstborn) and initiate a contract with them to legally adopt their child. This may sound unthinkable to us, but understand that in a culture that was all about climbing social ladders, this practice created a win-win situation. The family adopting the child secured a male heir, and the family giving up a child received a substantial payment *and* a permanent alliance with a powerful family. The point here is this: one did not adopt a child without paying a high price.

Third, as we've stated already, the purpose of Roman adoption was to secure an heir to whom would belong every right and privilege (as well as every denarius) associated with the family name. In other words, there was no qualitative difference between an adoptive child and a biological child. Once the adoption contract was completed, the adopted child's status was immediately changed. He received a new name and with that name a new identity and a new inheritance.

Finally, once an adoption was final, it was irrevocable. In the Roman Empire a legal process existed by which parents could disown and disinherit their biological children; however, once a family adopted a child, that child could never be legally disowned. His new identity was permanent and unassailable.

All this is a far cry from our modern "second-best" understanding of adoption. Adoptive children in the Roman Empire must have felt like they won the lottery! In fact, the first three emperors of Rome were adopted *so* they could be the emperors of Rome. Can you imagine? "You're adopted," was not an insult (another sitcom cliché: "Mom says you're adopted," as a way of putting down a sibling). It was a badge of honor, a windfall, a life-changing gift. That's how we're supposed to feel when we read Jesus' words here. That's how he meant it. That's how the disciples heard it. That's how John's readers read it. And I can tell you from personal experience that's exactly what adoption is.

My wife and I have the privilege of being the parents of three beautiful, adopted children. As such, I can't even begin to tell you how moving and meaningful Jesus' words are for us. We got married young and decided we would wait a while to have kids. We wanted some time just to be young, to settle into and enjoy married life, to build our careers, to sleep in. But after five years of marriage, we still didn't feel like we were ready to have kids. We started wondering if maybe we weren't the type to have kids.

Then it started to happen: Some friends of ours started an adoption process, then another couple. Pretty soon, we started seeing adoptions everywhere. On a road trip with one of my friends who was in the process of adopting, I asked him the classic question, "So why are you adopting? Could you not have 'your own kids'?"

He overlooked the ignorant way I asked the question and simply responded, "No, we can have biological children, but we feel like God is inviting us to make this our Plan A." Somewhat confused—I had never heard anything like this before—I asked him what he meant, so he continued, "Have you ever read what the Bible says about orphans and vulnerable children?" And right then and there, he walked me through Scripture from start to finish and showed me God's heart for adoption. Then he painted a picture on a global and local scale of the need and concluded with a mind-blowing statement. "If every third church (not every third Christian, every third church) in the United States adopted one child, there would be no more orphans in the foster system. If one in every twenty Christians globally took in one child, there would be no more orphans in the world."

This single conversation started a journey for me and for my wife that led us to a place where we both clearly heard the voice of God tell us, "I want you to build your family through adoption. I want that to be your Plan A. I want your home to be a place where orphans become daughters and sons." Within a year, we were holding our two adopted daughters in our arms. Several years after that, our adopted son. And I say all this to tell you conclusively, they are our kids. The first time we held them, we were theirs and they were ours. There is no qualitative difference between our kids and biological children.

We talk about adoption in front of our kids often. We invite them into the beauty of it at every opportunity. We offer it to them as a badge of honor. We tell them, "You are our Plan A. We chose you. You are immensely valuable to us. There was a lot we had to go through to adopt you—a lot of bureaucracy, a lot of waiting, a lot of emotions, a lot of prayer, a lot of uncertainty—and you were worth all of it. Everything we have is yours: our name, our resources, our home, our lives. And nothing anywhere will ever change that. We love you with all of our hearts, and we always will."

Listen to the voice of Jesus to his disciples, and to you, "I will not leave you as orphans; I will come to you." What he's saying is, "I chose you. I paid a high price for you. Everything I have is yours. And I will never change my mind." And this, as Jesus said in John 14, is why the Holy Spirit comes to us. This is what his arrival in our hearts and our communities means. It means we are so loved by God that he sends us his Spirit to confirm in us the identity Jesus won for us through his life, death, and resurrection. The Holy Spirit is the Spirit of adoption. The power in "empowered" is the power of adoption. The apostle Paul makes this abundantly clear in some of the most wonderful words ever written:

> For those who are led by the Spirit of God are the children of God. The Spirit you received does not make you slaves, so that you live in fear again; rather, the Spirit you received brought about your adoption to sonship. And by him we cry, "Abba, Father." The Spirit himself testifies with our spirit that we are God's children. Now if we are children, then we are heirs— heirs of God and co-heirs with Christ, if indeed we share in

his sufferings in order that we may also share in his glory.
(Romans 8:14–17)

It's all there, everything we've just talked about. God's Plan A was to bring us into his family, at a high cost, which results in a complete change in identity. And as Romans 8 goes on to show, nothing "in all of creation" can change any of it.

It's easy to get caught up in conversations about the manifestations of and workings of the Holy Spirit in the Bible and the church. It's understandable that sometimes we get into debates about what he's like and what kinds of things he does (or doesn't) do. It's only natural that when we are talking about someone who is known as the "wind of God,"[5] there might be some confusion about what he looks like and what he does. And I think God has grace for all our confusion (if only we could learn to have the same grace for one another), but he also doesn't want us to live in that confusion forever.

That's why he has given us John 14 and Romans 8, to distill all the Holy Spirit's work in Scripture and throughout history into this clear picture: he is the Spirit of love sent by the Son of love (who had himself been sent by the Father of love) to adopt us into this beautiful family that has love as its defining attribute and vocation.

At this point you might be thinking, "I understand the Father sending Jesus, and I understand that Jesus came and lived and died and rose again. And I think I see how these things make a way for us to be a part of God's family. But how does the Holy Spirit fit into this picture of adoption? What does he bring to the table that hasn't already been accomplished by the will of the Father and the obedience of the Son?" To answer that, we go back to John 14 and the Greek *parakletos*.

If you've studied a second language, you likely have encountered a word that cannot be translated with a single word but instead must be explained as a concept or, better yet, an image. *Parakletos* is one such word. For this reason, it has been the subject of much study and debate throughout the history of the church. The various translations of the Bible illustrate this struggle. Depending on the version of Scripture you pick up, you will read *parakletos* as "Counselor," "Helper," "Comforter," "Guide," "Friend," or "Advocate." Each of these translations has value in helping us understand the person of the Holy Spirit and his role in our lives and churches, but the one that most captures my attention and most accurately translates the essence of the Greek word is the last one: "Advocate."[6]

Parakletos is a compound word joining together two Greek words. First, *para*, which is a preposition meaning "alongside." The second word is the verb, *kaleo*, which means "to call." When we put these together, we have the Holy Spirit described as someone who "calls alongside." This definition in itself may or may not be helpful, but when we look at usage of the word outside of the Bible, we see it generally appears in the context of legal proceedings. It is a technical word describing an appointed representative who "calls out alongside" someone in a trial. In other words, a *parakletos* is a defense attorney or an "advocate."

This raises a question: "Then what does that make me? I thought we were talking about adoption, and suddenly I'm a defendant? I'm on trial?"

Remember, adoption is a legal proceeding. And in any legal matter, there is always the opportunity for multiple parties to present their perspectives. We have already established God's perspective, embodied in the person of Jesus: he loves us and welcomes us with open arms into his family. But there is another perspective in play. In Revelation 12, after a decisive battle had taken place, a loud voice in heaven announced:

> Now have come the salvation and the power and the kingdom of our God, and the authority of his Messiah. For the accuser of our brothers and sisters, who accuses them before our God day and night, has been hurled down. (Revelation 12:10)

"Accuser" is the literal meaning of the Hebrew word *satan*. It is not a proper name but a title; he is not "Satan" but "the satan," the accuser. It is a word that both describes his character and defines the limits of his power. What he does—and all he is able to do—is stand before the throne of God and call out accusations against everyone beloved by God and adopted into his family.

So as the adoption proceeding is wrapping up and all the paperwork is about to be signed, the accuser walks into the room and says, "Wait. Are you sure about this one? Don't you know what he's done? Can't you see how she's fallen short? How can you possibly think this one deserves to be a part of your family?"

The bad news is the accusations are true. As Paul tells us in Romans 3:23, we all fall short of the standard when the standard is the glory of God. So the accuser's indictments against us are not entirely unwarranted. But that's not the whole story; there is also good news—*the* Good News.

Also in Romans, back in chapter 8, Paul tells us there is someone else in the room who stands between us and any accusations.

> Christ Jesus who died—more than that, who was raised to life—is at the right hand of God and is also interceding for us. (Romans 8:34)

In response to the accusations against us, Jesus simply stands, raises his nail-scarred hands, and says, "Yes, but this one's mine." And with that, all accusation is silenced, condemnation is condemned, and the adoption is finalized.

What does this have to do with the Holy Spirit? In that scenario, according to Romans 8, *Jesus* is our advocate, *Jesus* is the one calling out alongside us. What is the Holy Spirit's role in all of this? If he is also our "advocate," to whom does he advocate? Once again, Romans 8 provides valuable insight:

> For those who are led by the Spirit of God are the children of
> God. The Spirit you received does not make you slaves, so that
> you live in fear again; rather, the Spirit you received brought
> about your adoption to sonship. And by him we cry, "Abba,
> Father." The Spirit himself testifies with our spirit that we are
> God's children. (Romans 8:14–16)

I think the accuser knows how the adoption hearing is going to end.
Maybe he didn't see it coming the first time, but now that he's seen it
play out over and over, he's under no illusions that he can condemn
anyone Jesus has redeemed. The voice of the accuser is never louder in
the Father's ears than the voice of his beloved Son. He will never win
that argument.

But maybe the accuser's airing of grievances is not simply about
God hearing what he has to say. There is, after all, someone else in
the room listening to his accusations. We are. The accuser is just as
interested in your hearing the condemnation he brings against you.
He knows there's nothing he can do to stop our adoption from going
through, but if he can make his voice louder in our ears than the
voice of Jesus, he can prevent us from living into the new identity
we've been given.

You see, it's one thing to be adopted, to be chosen, given a new
name, a new inheritance, and a new destiny. It's another thing
entirely to believe it and act like it's true.

Over years of living as orphans, we all developed habits that
made sense for our identities—ways of navigating the world around
us, ways of coping with the reality of our situations. And the muscle
memory of those coping mechanisms still exists even after our
adoption has been finalized.

Almost every adoptive parent, particularly if they have adopted
older children, has a heartbreaking story of their child's struggle to
believe they are actually safe, loved, and will be provided for. Many
adopted children continue to live out behaviors that made sense

in their old life even though they now have a new life and a new identity. The pantry in their new house is full, but they still hide food in their room because some part of them still believes there's not enough. They have a soft, warm bed in their new room, but they choose to sleep on the floor in the closet because that's what they've known. They know their new parents won't punish them for minor mistakes, but they still lie almost instinctively out of a learned need for self-protection. They have been adopted, but deep down they still believe they're orphans, so they continue to act like orphans. They have not yet accepted or begun to live into the new identity they have received.

This is exactly what the accuser intends. He wants his voice in our head: "Are you *sure* he chose you? You know what you've done. You know how you've fallen short. How can you possibly think you deserve to be a part of his family?" He wants us to question our adoption, our new identity. He wants us to keep returning to the ways of life that made sense before, to keep thinking and acting like orphans.

And his strategy works. We hear those words and internalize them. Pretty soon it's not him (or anyone else) speaking them over us. We now hear the accusations in our own voice. We have owned his condemnation. We have become our own accusers, and in doing so, we disqualify ourselves from the new identity and new destiny into which the Father has adopted us.

This is where the Holy Spirit comes in. He does not come to us to adopt us. That work has already been done through Jesus' life, death, and resurrection. The Holy Spirit comes, instead, to remind us of our adoption, to confirm and seal it in us.

Paul says God's Spirit "testifies *with our spirit* that we are God's children."[7] Did you catch that? The *parakletos*, the Advocate, comes to advocate *for us, to us.* When the voice of accusation rises up from our own spirit, he responds with the voice of Jesus, "Yes, but you're mine." He calls out alongside us, "Remember who you are! Those voices you're hearing, those words you're speaking over yourself, they used to be true of you but not anymore. In Christ, you are a new creation. The old has gone. The new has come."[8]

And he doesn't simply do this one time. Jesus said the Holy Spirit would come to us and stay with us "forever."[9] We had years (for some of us, decades) of accumulating habits and coping mechanisms prior to our adoption, so he comes to us for a lifetime to help us unlearn them so we can learn to live as his children, adopted and dearly loved.

All of this is the foundation of the empowered life. In order to experience and use this gift of power correctly, we need first to seek to understand the character of the Giver, who he is and what he is doing in our lives and the world. The quintessence of his character is love. He expresses that love by adopting us through Jesus, and he sends us the presence and power of the Holy Spirit to be for us the continual presence of his adoptive love in our lives. This is what the power in "empowered" is all about. This is what God is doing in us and in the world through us. This is what he invites us into through the power and presence of his Holy Spirit.

This understanding must shape how we seek, experience, and use his power. Our guiding image will always be adoption, our driving impulse always love. As we hear voices speaking identity over us, we will discern whether they are the voice of God (because, in all the noise, sometimes it's difficult to tell) by asking, "Is it loving?" This doesn't always mean is it soft, easy, or comfortable—true love is seldom any of those things—but rather is it consistent with the identity Jesus has given us? Is it calling us deeper into whom he adopted us to be? When we interact with one another in Christian community, with our sisters and brothers, adopted alongside us into the same family, we will seek to partner with the voice of the Holy Spirit, who is also their Advocate, and join him in calling out alongside them, "Remember who you are. You are his. You are loved." When we move through a broken and hurting world, we will cultivate an awareness that he is with us, we will listen to his voice on behalf of the people we meet every day, we will watch for the ways he is at work in the world, and we will make ourselves available to partner with him in that work, relying always on his presence and power at work in and through our lives.

Each of our three kids came to us with only one set of clothes. Mismatched, ill-fitting hand-me-downs that someone dug out of a donation box. Our son wasn't even wearing shoes when we met him, just a single sock. So the first thing my wife and I did with each child was to take them shopping and buy them a closet full of new clothes. We weren't trying to teach them materialism or show them how wealthy we are. We just didn't want them wearing orphan clothes anymore. We didn't want them to think of themselves as orphans. They had a family. They were safe. They would be taken care of. They were loved. They always would be. We immediately took their old clothes and put them in a box in the closet. The only thing they were good for anymore was a keepsake, a memento to mark their journey, a testimony of God's faithfulness in their lives.

Friend, don't go back to your orphan clothes, except to tell the story of God's faithfulness in your life. You are a daughter of the King, chosen and dearly loved. You are a son of God, adopted at a high price. He has made you an heir to his kingdom. He loves you, and he always will.[10]

He also knows you will forget who you are from time to time. He understands you will lose sight of what you're here to do. He is not surprised when you settle for less than the identity, family, and destiny into which he adopted you. That's why he has sent you a gift, an Advocate, who walks alongside you and calls out to you, "Remember who you are. There is more for you. You are his. You are loved."

This is and must always be the starting place of any conversation about the power of the Holy Spirit.

1

EMPOWERED HEART

Foundation - Josh Harrison

. . . .

The most important concept in this book is that the Holy Spirit is the Spirit of adoption sent by the Father to bring us into relationship with him. The second most important concept follows naturally: you have a part to play in that relationship. An empowered life is not something that happens to you; a vibrant relationship always requires two willing parties.

One of the places we tend to misstep when thinking and talking about the Holy Spirit is when we use language like "filled" and "baptized." There is nothing inherently wrong with these words; in fact, they are straight out of the Bible. The problem arises when we use these words outside the context of a relationship.

Remember, the Bible reveals to us a God who chooses to walk with, talk with, identify himself with, and work through people. From start to finish, the Bible is the story of this relational God. For the New Testament writers, Pentecost and everything that followed in the life of the early Church was the continuation of that story.

The story starts with Yahweh walking and talking with Adam and Eve, as friends do. There is certainly a hierarchy in place: he is God, and they are not. At the same time, he treated them with respect, as friends. He honored their sovereignty. He gave them a choice.

One of the enduring questions of the creation story is: Why did God put the Tree of Knowledge of Good and Evil in the garden at all? I think the answer is exactly what we're talking about here. He put that particular tree in the garden and pointed it out to them because he values relationship, and true relationship always requires an act of will from both parties. For love to exist, we must be able to choose. True love requires vulnerability on the part of the one extending it. It exposes us to the possibility that our love will be rejected. God so deeply valued the relationship with Adam and Eve (and all of us) that he allows us to *choose* even if (and when) we choose to walk away.

As the story continues, we see this God choose a family as his own. He appears to them and speaks to them directly, blessing them, protecting them, and guiding them. In Genesis 16, one of the most startling moments in the whole Bible, Yahweh stops the whole arc of Scripture to rescue and bless a foreign slave girl named Hagar. He is a God of relationship, a God who cares about people.

In Exodus 3, when Moses, the chosen rescuer of God's enslaved people, approached the burning bush, God introduced himself as "the God of Abraham, the God of Isaac, and the God of Jacob" (Exod. 3:15). Before He even provided his name, Yahweh, he provided relational context. He identified himself by *their* names.

And all of this is just in the first few pages of Scripture.

We could go on to speak of judges, kings, priests, and prophets— women and men— who entered the story as ordinary people but were made extraordinary through their relationship with God.

Finally, we meet the New Testament writers, many of whom spent more than three years walking around with the person they had come to understand was God himself. They had seen him face-to-face, eaten with him, and talked with him as a friend. They had experienced intimacy with God in ways the patriarchs never could have imagined. It was in this context—the context of a God of relationship who is intimately and powerfully involved in the lives of his people—that they used words like "filled with the Holy Spirit" and "baptized in the Holy Spirit." They knew they were writing the next chapter in the same story, the story of a God of relationship.

The earliest Christians saw themselves not as a new movement but as the expansion of this relationship to all people and all nations. It was always about relationship. They were being filled by a person. They were being baptized—immersed in and fundamentally changed by—the love of a person.

"Filled" and "baptized." These are powerful and important words. But they become problematic when we forget the backstory and begin to use them transactionally rather than relationally. When we do so, we depersonalize the Holy Spirit, thinking of him as a force rather than a person. (Think about it for a moment. If you've been around the church for a while, how many times have you heard the Holy Spirit referred to as "it" rather than "him"?) We speak of wind and water—again, biblical images—but forget these are descriptions of a person, of his character and work in the world and our lives.

The result is all sorts of bizarre behavior, and even worse, division in the church as we squabble over when, how, how often, and whether a person is "filled by the Holy Spirit." How silly do these arguments sound when we realize we are talking about a relationship with a person? We would never talk this way about a friend. "I believe I received my friend fully when we first met." What a sad friendship if that were true! Or, on the other hand, "I believe I need a second encounter with my friend to receive him completely." Really? Just one more? I love the way Terry Virgo talks about this. When asked if he believes in the "second filling" of the Holy Spirit, he responds, "Oh, yes! It comes right after the first filling and right before the third."[11] This is how relationships work.

Meaningful relationships are not transactional but are ongoing encounters with another person you will *never* reach the end of because that person is unique and complex and endlessly interesting. If this is true of our relationships with one another, how much more so when the other person is God himself! We do not need one or even two encounters with him. What we need—and what he offers—is a lifelong journey of knowing and growing. When we reduce the Holy Spirit to a baptizing substance or a filling force, we depersonalize him and, in doing so, settle for less than the real, vibrant relationship for which he has come to us.

Of course, when we depersonalize him, we also depersonalize ourselves. No longer are we people in relationship with a person; we are instead objects being filled by, immersed in, or acted upon by a force. We begin to refer to ourselves as vessels to be filled or rooms to be occupied. Yes, these are good, biblical pictures, but we must be careful to use them as the writers of the Bible and the Holy Spirit who inspired those writers intended. The problem with both images is that they convey passivity when divorced from relationship. Neither a vessel nor a room has a will. Both are filled whether they like it or not. But this is not how the Holy Spirit works.

Remember the second most important concept in this book: we have a part to play in our relationship with the Holy Spirit. Filling and empowerment are not done *to* us. They are done *with* us. The Holy Spirit invites. He does not override.

In one of the most famous and important verses about life with the Holy Spirit, Paul writes: "Do not get drunk on wine, which leads to debauchery. Instead, be filled with the Spirit" (Eph. 5:18). Yes, the language seems to indicate a vessel or an empty room, and indeed the verb tense used here is passive (meaning that the subject, "you," is being acted upon by the object, "the Holy Spirit"), but what's interesting about this particular verb is that it is not only passive but also imperative. It is a command: "You be filled." In other words, for this verse to work, it requires agency from both parties. The Holy Spirit wills to fill us, and we must will to be filled.

The comparison with drunkenness is an enlightening one here. No one can be drunk without alcohol, but no one can blame alcohol for making them drunk. They chose to drink. Likewise, without the

Holy Spirit, we can do nothing. We cannot live this empowered life without his choosing to fill us with his presence and power, but he will not fill us unless we choose to be filled. As Augustine is reputed to have said, "Without God, we cannot. Without us, God will not."[12] Ephesians 5 might sound impersonal at first reading (subject and object) but understood rightly, it is about two people choosing a relationship with one another. It is every bit as intimate and moving as Romans 8.

How do we choose relationship? How do we will to be filled? We must begin by emptying ourselves. In John 15, Jesus told his disciples:

> I am the vine; you are the branches. If you remain in me and I in you, you will bear much fruit; apart from me you can do nothing. (John 15:5)

We must take him seriously.

We love that verse until it's time to live like it's true. When it comes down to it, many of us act as if Jesus were being hyperbolic. Sure, "spiritually" we're lost apart from him, but we can do plenty of things without him. Or we just need him for the really big stuff when we're in over our heads. (I call this "Carrie Underwood theology"— you know, "Jesus, take the wheel.")[13] Or worse still, we need a little bit of him, a hit or a sprinkle of Jesus, to get us through our day. We need him when we *need* him, but for the most part, our lives are manageable without him.

In fact, I've even heard many Christians inadvertently reverse the order. The famous line by Teresa of Ávila, "Christ has no body now but yours," is an example of this reversal. I understand what St. Teresa was saying, and there is certainly meaningful, biblical truth here. But if we're not careful, we'll take this to mean that Jesus really needs us if he's going to get anything done, as if John 15:5 says, "Apart from us, he can do nothing."

We must disabuse ourselves of the notion that we are basically okay on our own. Self-actualization is not the path to happiness; we do not simply need to "find our truth" to experience fulfillment. You see, contrary to what almost everyone is telling us these days, our way doesn't work. We were born in and acculturated to a system enslaved to what the Bible calls "the powers," and consequently enslaved to our own coping mechanisms and ways of dealing with life under the powers, which the Bible calls "sin."

Paul reminds us in Ephesians 2:

> As for you, you were dead in your transgressions and sins, in which you used to live when you followed the ways of this world and of the ruler of the kingdom of the air, the spirit who is now at work in those who are disobedient. All of us also lived among them at one time, gratifying the cravings of our flesh and following its desires and thoughts. Like the rest, we were by nature deserving of wrath. But because of his great love for us, God, who is rich in mercy, made us alive with Christ even when we were dead in transgressions—it is by grace you have been saved. (Ephesians 2:1–5)

Many people today treat Jesus as a bonus add-on to what they consider to be an otherwise functional life, as if he is our cheerleader, emotional support system, or in-case-of-emergency contact. But God did not send his Son to die for us, nor does he send his Holy Spirit to empower us, simply to make a few minor tweaks and changes to an otherwise good life. The Bible and our own experience are clear on this: we need a Savior and Lord, someone to save us from the powers, save us from ourselves, and teach us to live in the freedom he has won for us. This is why Jesus came, and this is why he freely gives his Spirit. He came to make us new, to give us a new name, a new purpose, and new power.

But to receive all of this, we must be willing to give up our old identities, plans, and ways of functioning. We must be discontent with the status quo and long for "more." We must reject the notion that happiness comes through independence and instead learn the joy of deep dependence on the empowering presence of the Holy Spirit, without whom we can do *nothing*. We must come to him with open hands, with only our need to offer ourselves to him, and find him ready and willing to fill every inch of empty space with himself and with his abundant, overflowing, extravagant life.

In his book *Mere Christianity*, C. S. Lewis describes this beautifully:

> Imagine yourself as a living house. God comes in to rebuild that house. At first, perhaps, you can understand what He is doing. He is getting the drains right and stopping the leaks in the roof and so on; you knew that those jobs needed doing and so you are not surprised. But presently He starts knocking the house about in a way that hurts abominably and does not seem to make any sense. What on earth is He up to? The explanation is that He is building quite a different house from the one you thought of—throwing out a new wing here, putting on an extra floor there, running up towers, making courtyards. You thought you were being made into a decent little cottage: but He is building a palace. He intends to come and live in it Himself.[14]

The problem for most of us is that this kind of surrender to and dependence on the work of the Great Palace Builder doesn't come naturally. I know this is true for me. I'm an American. I grew up in a cultural context that celebrates *independence* as one of the highest virtues to which a human being can aspire. I was taught from an early age that I can do anything I put my mind to. And Western culture has told me the greatest good I can pursue is the actualization of my dreams by my power.

While I am profoundly grateful to have been born and raised in a country that values freedom and human sovereignty, this emphasis on independence can be remarkably handicapping when it comes to our relationships with the Holy Spirit. The kind of "apart from me, you can do nothing" dependence Jesus described in John 15 is completely foreign to us unless one of two things happens.

First, the wheels can fall off our otherwise smooth ride through life. Inevitably, we all encounter moments and extended seasons when we realize just how fragile our ability to control our lives actually is. We experience a loss of a family member or a friend, we receive a scary diagnosis, we lose a job, we lose a meaningful relationship.

Some people respond to this level of adversity by turning away from faith and relationship with God. Others, conversely, experience a much deeper sense of desperation and dependence as they walk through hardship, leaning fully into and on their relationship with God. With time, the latter often look back on seasons like these with a sense of both profound pain and profound joy—not bubbly, bouncing-off-the-walls joy, but the kind James meant when he wrote, "Consider it pure joy, my brothers and sisters, whenever you face trials of many kinds" (James 1:2). This is the joy of dependence.

My family and I have never prayed with such desperation or passion, nor have we known the presence of God with such clarity or power, as when we've walked through pain: when we were navigating the foster system with our son, when we felt betrayed by friends, when my dad passed away. These kinds of seasons come to all of us eventually. Depending on how we engage with them—do they drive us from God or to him?—these seasons can be productive in our lives. God, in his grace, redeems these times of pain by using them to produce in us dependence on his power and love.

But we do not need to wait for things to fall apart to learn dependence. We can also cultivate it through daily discipline. We will discuss this more in the next chapter, but many of the spiritual disciplines God has given us are what we call "disciplines of abstinence"—things we stop doing. These disciplines of abstinence—practices such as fasting, observing the Sabbath, tithing, and experiencing silence and solitude—are incredibly countercultural. They help us resist the "natural" culture of self-centered independence in favor of learning the kingdom culture of dependence on the empowering Spirit of God. As we practice these disciplines, we intentionally choose weakness in ourselves so we can experience the fullness of his power at work in and through us.

One of the most moving scenes in the Bible is found in Luke 15. A father sees his lost boy returning home, runs down the road to meet him, and wraps him in a father's embrace before the son can even say a word. This scene shows the lengths to which the Father himself will go (and has gone) to restore us to relationship with him. But the rest of the story tells us that none of it would have happened if the son hadn't gotten tired of the pig pen.

Friends, God has more for us. I say that confidently to anyone regardless of their spiritual maturity. When we are talking about being in an empowering relationship with an infinite God, there is always more. But remember, he will only fill what you will give.

Bridge - Todd Proctor

This call to be surrendered to and filled by the Holy Spirit is not just a one-time encounter, but an ongoing, life-giving, and empowering relationship that is new ground for many. This includes not only those who have grown up in the church, but those who now lead it.

I have met countless pastors with a background similar to mine: raised in faith communities and cultures with very little emphasis or expectancy toward the work of the Spirit.

Others carry a charismatic heritage that has sometimes held them back or scared them off. Discomfort, anxiety, or even trauma from past experiences labeled as the movement of the Spirit (often steeped in hype or emotional manipulation) can be a powerful deterrent to experiencing the real thing.

My friend Harvey Carey, founding pastor of Citadel of Faith in Detroit, Michigan, has lived this story. Here he tells his story of coming back home to fresh intimacy and expectancy in his relationship with the Spirit. As he shares his journey, I'm reminded of the timeless but true adage, "You can't lead others where you haven't been." I not only witnessed Harvey's "homecoming" moment in London years ago but have seen the ripple effects since then. God has used Harvey to ignite new expectancy in his church and city as well as the lives of leaders across the nation.

Frontiers – Harvey Carey

Harvey Carey is the planter and senior pastor of Citadel of Faith Church in Detroit, Michigan.

Unexpected. In a word, that's what my journey with the Holy Spirit has been.

I was raised in a single-parent household by a mother who was a strong woman of faith. I was required to recite Bible verses before beginning any meal. Bedtime was preceded by prayers. The inner-city Baptist church we attended hosted an infinitely full calendar of teas, concerts, and church services that often lasted for hours. I was a tenor in the choir and frequently spoke for special events. We never missed a Sunday.

Over time, spiritual ideas and activities became inseparably woven into the fabric of my life. But the truth is, although I had a cognitive understanding of the deity of Christ, was actively engaged in a church, and had a Catholic and Jesuit school education, I could not claim a personal relationship with Jesus.

I knew the Christian faith held to the doctrine of the Trinity, God in three persons: Father, Son, and Holy Spirit. I had become very familiar and somewhat comfortable with a basic understanding of the Father, who longs to reunite with fallen humanity and included prophets, sacrificial systems, and covenant promises in his plan to one day restore the broken union between himself and mankind. I also knew God's only Son, Jesus, became the bridge that would restore the relationship between fallen humanity and Holy God by sacrificing his life and blood. But the mystery of the third person of the Trinity— the Holy Spirit—remained elusive to me.

My first introduction to the person and work of the Holy Spirit occurred in the small Baptist church of my childhood. There were long, passionate sermons. Goosebumps were plentiful every time our choir belted out a song that stirred the soul. And almost every time the Hammond B-3 organ began to play, people would jump up from their seats like popcorn. Some would shout, others would run around the church as if doing laps on a track, and still others would begin to dance in sync with the organ music. Tears would flow, some people would fall into a coma-like state, and others would literally lose their wigs in their ecstatic praise to God.

I remember asking my mother during one of these moments, "Mommy, what's going on with these people?" Her answer gave me my first introduction to the person and work of the Holy Spirit. My mom replied, "Baby, they caught the Holy Ghost."

Almost as curious was what those same people did when the music ended: they came to an immediate, abrupt stop. I thought to myself, *If they caught the Holy Ghost, I don't want to catch it.* They also must have thrown him back because their actions stopped when the music stopped. *Give me the Father and give me Jesus, but the Ghost guy . . . not so much.*

As I moved through Jesuit prep school, I became even fonder of the work of the Father to bring people back to himself and the amazing work and example of Jesus, the ultimate servant. Yet with all of this knowledge, there was still an emptiness in my heart that nothing seemed to fill.

I applied to several colleges, was accepted by all, and chose to attend Northwestern University. I was granted an internship at one of the nation's leading financial institutions and guaranteed a job (upon completing college) in the top tier of a flagship bank in the heart of Chicago's financial district. I knew I had much to be thankful for and was thrilled to begin at Northwestern, but the nagging feeling of emptiness remained an undercurrent beneath the surface of my life.

I didn't know it then, but everything was about to change. Northwestern would be the catalyst for the empty space to be filled.

One night my soul was particularly unsettled. I left a party on campus with my thoughts full of some of the biggest questions I've ever had. *What was the meaning of life? Why did I feel so empty when I had so much? Who is God anyway? What's my purpose?* These and other soul-wrenching questions had been haunting me like a specter and now had come to stare me down.

I remember going back to my dorm and contemplating a very dark idea that had been steeping in my mind. Having struggled with depression for years as a child, this current season of emptiness had brought me to the ultimate dark place.

I headed back out into the cool, cloudy autumn night. By the time I reached the spot I had in mind, I had resolved that my life was no longer worth living. I assessed my surroundings and decided my planned suicide attempt had a strong probability of success: a high-elevation bridge, a dangerous drop to sharp rocks beneath, and I couldn't swim.

But first, I did the last desperate thing I knew to do. I called out to the God I had heard about, sung about, read about, and admired from a distance. I remember saying, "If you're all-knowing, then you know what I'm getting ready to do. If you are who you say you are, you need to intervene now."

Presenting ultimatums to the Almighty is not a recommended approach. Nonetheless, I cried out. And he heard me! That night Jesus became my Lord and Savior, and my life changed.

Back at my dormitory, I threw out every poster and mixtape that was not God-honoring. Then I picked up a zippered King James Bible I had received as a graduation gift from elementary school. Much to my roommate's bewilderment, I spent the next two days continuously reading this newly discovered treatise on God and his love for me and the world around me. I wept, laughed, rejoiced, worshiped, and came to know God in a way I had never thought I would.

I had to share this Good News with somebody, so I began hosting daily Bible studies at the African American Student Affairs building. Knowing little about conducting a Bible study, I simply shared what I had learned about God through the Bible. Not only did students come, but they came back again and again, and even more joined them. I said to God, "I could do this all the time!"

And I heard the Lord say to me, "You will!"

Although I now had a personal relationship with God, the Holy Spirit remained largely an enigma. Thanks to a series of short books I had discovered that were written by charismatic authors, my impressions of the Holy Spirit now included not just goosebumps, but also tongues, prophetic utterances, healing, and miracles. I no longer feared the erratic behavior I had observed in my childhood church, but neither had I personally connected with the unfamiliar "gifts of the Spirit." (I realize now that I had very little information about the "fruit" the Holy Spirit gives that develops our character, but instead I had a proliferation of writings on the gifts and even more pronounced "power gifts.")

I joined a newly founded church where I continued to grow in my faith and calling to full-time ministry. At an annual church retreat, I met the Holy Spirit in yet another unexpected way. Hundreds had gathered to learn the Word of God and express worship to the King of kings. Once again, a Hammond B-3 organ provided the soundtrack for a passionate time of worship. As people around me danced and shouted, I prayed, "God, I want to give you the praise you so rightfully deserve, but I'm not sure I can do it the way they are." And then I said, "Holy Spirit, I surrender to you."

My next realization was the room had emptied, and I was lying face down on the floor. I had been speaking to God for over two hours in a language I had never learned. This was the spiritual gift of tongues—one of those power gifts I had so vehemently avoided and feared. Suddenly, I had it, and it became a regular part of my conversations with God.

This new element of my relationship with the Holy Spirit gave me a hunger to know even more about him and his ministry, gifts, and fruit. At the same time, some shifts in my ministry began creating unwanted distance in my relationship with him.

I spent the next several years pursuing training and education in Dallas, Texas. The churches I attended and the ministers who became my mentors adopted a posture of respect and acknowledgment of the Holy Spirit. But there were very few expressions of his work and life in worship services, discipleship programs, or everyday life. My already-skewed sensitivity to how "creepy" the Holy Spirit might seem to those who didn't know him grew even more distorted. My encounters with the Holy Spirit became increasingly private and something I shared with others less.

Even as these changes occurred, I was aware they went against everything I saw in Scripture. I marveled at the way the Holy Spirit encouraged, endowed, and performed miracles that pointed so many to Jesus. Far from being creepy, the Holy Spirit seemed to be a normal and expected person in the life of the early church. By restraining my relationship with him, I was unknowingly doing what Ephesians 4:30 warned against: "grieving the Holy Spirit of God."

In 2003, I planted Citadel of Faith Covenant Church in Detroit, Michigan. Many unchurched, de-churched, and seekers came to faith and to our family, and our church became a multicultural community that expressed the beautiful complexities of our multifaceted God. Because we specifically wanted to be a welcoming place for those who had previously experienced hurt or confusion through a church, we intentionally avoided many of the more "peculiar" aspects of church culture at large.

I had no idea I was unwittingly creating an atmosphere where we were not allowing the Holy Spirit to exercise his full power in us and through us. I didn't know what we were missing—until I was invited to a meeting in London to learn about a new evangelism movement called Alpha.

Curious and eager to learn, I crossed the Atlantic to gather with other American pastors at Holy Trinity Brompton Church. In recent years Alpha had seen an unprecedented number of people from all walks of life throughout England come to a saving relationship with Jesus. Alpha's leaders wanted to share with us what they had learned so we, too, could reach more people throughout our own country. They said the most significant work of Alpha didn't come from programming, packaging, or leaders' knowledge. Instead, the "secret sauce" was in creating a safe place to ask questions, pray, and invite the movement of the Holy Spirit.

There he was again, the Holy Spirit, being mentioned with such normalcy and non-weirdness that I immediately leaned in.

Those few days in England once again refined my view of and relationship with the Holy Spirit. In particular, I'll never forget a moment set aside to do something unfamiliar to most of us. We were all invited to open our hands as if waiting to receive a present, and simply to say:

"Come, Holy Spirit."

This seemed innocent enough. Yet it became the gateway for my second pivotal meeting with the person of the Godhead I had been avoiding for so many years. This simple posture and prayer not only paved the way for revival in my soul but in my church as well. No band, no lights to set the mood, no oil applied, or hands placed on anyone. Simply an opening of my own hands and lifting of my voice to speak to him:

"Come, Holy Spirit."

He did. And I met him again. But this time I felt no fear, no shame—just an open heart and soul for the Holy Spirit to come into any way he chose. The tongues I had so often suppressed rolled once again off these lips of clay to the Potter who was doing his work on the vessel called Harvey's life. I lay prostrate before him and didn't care what anyone thought. I repented for years of fear of trusting the Holy Spirit to do the ministry he's been sent to do in my life and the life of my church.

Today I remain committed to not making any of God's work, person, and ministry "weird." However, I will no longer grieve the Holy Spirit of God. I returned to Detroit with renewed purpose and fervor to invite, expect, and welcome the one who wants to empower, comfort, teach, administer, help, intercede, heal, develop, and seal us into the life of the church and relationship with him.

Are you a skeptic, wounded, or ambivalent? I ask you to consider a new way of thinking about the member of the Godhead most of us rarely speak to, let alone allow to influence our lives or ministries. With open hands and heart, invite him to be active in all parts of your life. I implore you, yes, even dare you to pray:

"Come, Holy Spirit!"

REFLECTION QUESTIONS

1. Reflect on your past church experiences and formation as a
   believer. How were you taught to relate to the Holy Spirit?
   What was missing or rarely discussed? How do you think
   your perspective affected your formation and development as a
   Christ follower?

2. How has your relationship with the Holy Spirit of God operated
   to define and shape (limit or expand) your ministry so far in your
   life? What has the impact been on you, on your circles of family
   and friends, and on your church?

3. Our relationship with the Holy Spirit is a lifelong endeavor
   of growing in love. What will it take for you to grow in your
   relationship with him? What are the potential outcomes or
   consequences of remaining in your current relationship with the
   Holy Spirit?

4. What is preventing you from trusting the Holy Spirit with open
   hands and inviting him—*"Come, Holy Spirit"*—to do the ministry
   he has been sent to do?

2

EMPOWERED LIFE

Foundation – Josh Harrison

. . . .

In the last chapter, we discussed how this empowering relationship with the Holy Spirit is not something that is done to us but rather something in which we must be active participants. He will only fill what we will give him.

In this chapter, we will see that this act of giving ourselves, this posture of surrender to and dependence on the Holy Spirit, is not a one-time encounter or a secondary experience; it is a daily choice. Like any other relationship, our relationship with God requires an ongoing commitment to growth in knowledge and intimacy. In fact, a verse we discussed in the preceding chapter has further insight for us:

> Do not get drunk on wine, which leads to debauchery. Instead, be filled with the Spirit. (Ephesians 5:18)

Previously, we noted that the verb phrase "be filled" is both passive and imperative, meaning that both the person being filled and the person doing the filling have a part to play. The Holy Spirit fills: we cannot do it without him. We choose to be filled: he will not do it without us.

However, what we didn't mention in the previous chapter is that the *passive* imperative verb is also a *present* imperative verb which, in Greek, carries a sense of ongoing action. In other words, the command here is not simply to be filled with the Holy Spirit once, but to "go on being filled" with the Spirit.

Again, if we are talking about a relationship, this makes sense. Who immediately after their wedding day would presume they have reached complete knowledge of their spouse? Who after one day with a new friend would say, "I have sounded the depths of their soul"? True intimacy is a lifelong journey that involves all sorts of choices and experiences along the way.

Our relationship with the Holy Spirit works the same way. It is not a binary proposition—not all in or all out. Real relationships are much more complex, much more dynamic. We can have been filled by him but still "grieve him" by the way we live. We can have experienced his adoption but still live as orphans. We can, as Paul instructs us, "walk in step with the Spirit,"[15] which of course means we can also know the Holy Spirit while walking out of step with him. In other words, we must choose him daily, choose to grow in knowledge and love. The question is not simply, "Do you believe in him?" but, "Do you know him?" Not, "Have you received him?" but, "Do you walk with him?"

I have a seven-year-old son. I've discovered there are times when I'm walking with him, but he's not walking with me. This is especially true as we pass the toy aisle at Target. We're holding hands heading somewhere together when something interesting catches his eye. Suddenly, we're no longer heading the same direction. I'm still holding his hand, but he's no longer holding mine.

Many of us act like my seven-year-old when it comes to our relationships with the Holy Spirit. We know he's got us. He has adopted us. We are no longer orphans. We have a new identity. We have a family. We have the promise of resurrection and his persistent presence as a deposit guaranteeing that inheritance. We are "saved," as we like to say, but we don't act like it.

He's holding onto us, but we're not holding onto him. We expect him to carry (or drag) us through this life and deliver us safe and sound at the gates of heaven where we will finally begin to live into this new name he has given us. This is not the vibrant relationship with the Holy Spirit and empowered life that is available to us. It is not a *mature* relationship.

In the preface, we spoke about Christian identity being formed through adoption. Through the will of the Father, the obedience of the Son, and the presence of the adoptive power of God, his Holy Spirit, we have become children of God. In Romans 8, Paul says the Holy Spirit empowers us to cry out to God as "Abba."[16] This is an Aramaic word that is technically translated "Father," but the technical translation only tells part of the story.

"Abba" is a simple word, with one long vowel and one soft consonant in a short, repeated pattern making it the perfect word for someone just learning to speak. Just like our English words "Mama" and "Dada," "Abba" is one of the first words a Jewish child would learn. It is an intimate word, one that's taught through proximity, learned through embrace.

Let's never lose sight of how amazing this is.

Once, in a conversation with a Jewish friend, I asked the question, "Do you think of God as your Father?"

The look of surprise on her face said it all. "No!" she replied. "He is the Creator, the Law-Giver, the God of heaven's armies, the Holy One of Israel. How could I ever presume such an intimate relationship with the Most High God?"

Yet that's exactly what God invites us to do. At the Father's initiative, by his will, he reaches out to us when we are far away and draws us near. Through obedience and sacrifice, Jesus gives us his relationship with the Father: a relationship of proximity, intimacy, and embrace. Through the ongoing presence and power of his Holy Spirit, we are invited into the closest possible relationship with the almighty God.

If this doesn't blow our minds on a regular basis, we're not really thinking about it! He has adopted us into his family. We can now relate to God as Abba, the way a little child relates to their loving daddy.

This doesn't mean, however, that he wants us to remain perpetually infantile in our relationship with him. Though he invites us into this kind of intimacy forever, though we can know him as "Abba" for a lifetime, that's not his only name. There are other ways we can experience him and relate to him as we grow into a more mature relationship with him. C. S. Lewis captures this brilliantly in a conversation between Aslan and Lucy in *The Chronicles of Narnia*:

> "Aslan," said Lucy, "you're bigger."
> "That is because you are older, little one," answered he.
> "Not because you are?"
> "I am not. But every year you grow, you will find me bigger."[17]

Though he stays the same, we do not. We grow. He wants us to grow in knowledge and experience of him *and* participation with him. He doesn't want to drag us through this life. While there will be times we still need him to carry us, he wants us to learn to walk *with* him.

As much as my wife and I have enjoyed and are enjoying our kids' childhoods, we did not adopt them so they could remain our "little ones" forever. The point of adopting, of parenting, is to grow adults with whom we can have mature relationships; who will have their own families that will live out, in unique ways, our family values and culture; who will carry on our legacy; and who will make an impact on the world around them.

In the same way, God has not adopted us so we can remain perpetual toddlers, but rather so we can grow into adults who approach him with intimacy and maturity; who invest in our own families of faith wherein we creatively express his values and culture; who embody his character, learned in intimacy, to everyone around us; and who engage in his work of reconciliation and restoration in the world. At some point, we should move from being consumers of grace to being participants with grace.

In Philippians 3, Paul puts it like this:

> Not that I have already obtained all this, or have already arrived at my goal, but *I press on to take hold of that for which Christ Jesus took hold of me.* Brothers and sisters, I do not consider myself yet to have taken hold of it. But one thing I do: Forgetting what is behind and straining toward what is ahead, I press on toward the goal to win the prize for which God has called me heavenward in Christ Jesus. *All of us, then, who are mature should take such a view of things.* And if on some point you think differently, that too God will make clear to you. Only let us live up to what we have already attained. (Philippians 3:12–16)

We see the picture clearly here. Jesus, Paul says, has already taken hold of us. He's got us, and there is nothing that can take us from his hand. But now it's time we take hold of him. He's holding our hand, but are we holding his? This, Paul reminds us, is not a one-time decision but an ongoing journey that requires commitment and effort: "press on," "straining toward," "live up to."

There is certainly an initial encounter where we first experience Jesus by his Spirit and bow to him as our Lord, but that moment is the beginning, not the end, of our journey. This walk with him is about daily surrender, daily working out and living into the implications of his lordship in our lives, daily following where his Spirit is leading us and becoming who he has (re)created us to be, and daily becoming who we already are.

This is what we mean when we say we want "more" of the Holy Spirit. It's not that the Holy Spirit is withholding parts of himself from us and demanding that we beg for more. The truth is rather that we are incapable of receiving more of him than we already have *unless* we grow and offer more of ourselves to him. Remember, he will only fill what we give.

The problem is that giving him everything is not as simple as singing a song or praying a prayer. None of us yet has what it takes to fully surrender ourselves to him. Indeed, many of us find it difficult to yield even an inch of our lives. None of us can, right now by direct effort, be and do everything God has recreated us in Jesus to be and do.

Much to our surprise and disappointment, the Holy Spirit does not simply snap his fingers and do all the work. Initially, it seems like he may do just that. After all, in the moment of our first encounter with him, he does miraculous work: taking us from lost to found, from oppressed to liberated, from orphan to daughter or son in the blink of an eye. Sometimes, people who encounter the love of God through the Holy Spirit describe the experience of chains being broken, long-entrenched habits no longer holding appeal, or destructive patterns suddenly losing their power. He does a great deal of work in us during that first meeting. But there is still plenty more to do.

Very quickly, we realize our lives are not yet heaven and we are not yet perfect. Our old lives are still waiting for us, and though we may have experienced significant deliverance, there are still parts of our identity and personality where we must "work out our own salvation." We have been set free, but now we must learn to live free.

How do we do that? We do it by practicing daily disciplines through which we cultivate habits of surrender, dependence, and growth. In doing so, we become active participants with the Holy Spirit in his work in us and the world around us. This longing for more of the Holy Spirit must be much more than a prayer we pray. It must become a lifestyle we live. In a maturing relationship with God, it is not enough simply to ask for "more." We must participate with him in that more.

Discussing our role in participating with the Holy Spirit through disciplines, Dallas Willard says this:

> A discipline in any area is something in my power that I do to enable me to do what I cannot do by direct effort. This is the general nature of discipline, and there is simply no area of human attainment—from playing a musical instrument, to sports, to speaking a language or being friendly—that does not require discipline.[18]

All of us learned our old identities through environment and repetition. Why would we think our new identities would be any different? In fact, given the amount of time we poured into those old identities, and that we are perhaps still living in the environments in which those identities were formed, it shouldn't surprise us that effort is required to unlearn many of the habits, coping mechanisms, and self-reliances we picked up along the way.

The Holy Spirit indeed does powerful, miraculous work in us when we first surrender ourselves to him and receive his adopting love. But he does not take us all the way to glory in that moment. Instead, he invites us into a journey on which we become active participants in our own formation. He invites us to partner with him in the work he is doing in our lives and the lives of those around us. The way we enter this partnership is not through big moments or grand gestures, but through small decisions made daily that continuously make us aware of his presence, attentive to his voice, and reliant on his power.

As in all good things, Jesus is our example. We know Jesus is the Son of God who came to earth for a season and lived among people. But it's important to recognize Jesus also lived that season as a man who experienced a similar environment and faced many of the challenges we face.

The book of Hebrews tells us, "For we do not have a high priest who is unable to empathize with our weaknesses, but we have one who has been tempted in every way, just as we are—yet he did not sin."[19] "He did not sin" simply means he did not choose coping mechanisms or distractions but rather fully embraced his identity and vocation as Son of God. He modeled a life of perfect surrender, dependence, and partnership in his Father's work.

How did he do it? He did it not in his own strength as the Son of God, but in the power of the Holy Spirit. The Gospel writers are all clear on this: Jesus was a man of the Spirit, who did everything he did—including rising from the dead—by the power of the same Spirit who is with us, in us, and who longs to make more of himself available to us as we make more of ourselves available to him.

How did Jesus come to this fully surrendered, fully empowered life? Through a life of discipline that cultivated his dependence on the Holy Spirit. Jesus was famous among his followers for his prayer life, for his pursuit of "alone time" with his Father, for his unhurried pace, for the simplicity of his lifestyle, and for many other daily habits that formed his identity as a man of the Spirit and empowered everything he did.

Yes, one could argue Jesus had knowledge and experience we do not have (existing in perfect relationship with the Holy Spirit before the foundation of the world, conceived by the Holy Spirit, etc.). And while this is certainly true, it doesn't take anything away from the point. In fact, it only strengthens it. If Jesus, who had access to these divine resources, still found it necessary to pursue a life of discipline to walk in the presence and power of the Holy Spirit, then how much more do *we* need to pursue his lifestyle if we also want to experience his power?

Bridge – Todd Proctor

As Josh describes embracing the lifestyle of Jesus to access the power of the Spirit, I admit I'm tempted to write this off as inspirational and aspirational, but not really sustainable. My journey with the Spirit has been marked by a number of encounter-fueled sprints. Make no mistake, I am grateful for awakening, mountaintop moments that remind me God is real and his presence is with and for me. Yet often these have not translated into sustained transformation.

Kathleen Doyle is a friend who has modeled a patient pursuit of the Spirit, which has carried her to and through dark valleys. As a pastor, she has helped shape and shepherd three very large church communities in Southern California. But it's her call as a therapist and counselor that has taught her to "count by ones" and mentor others in the slow work of spiritual disciplines for the sake of a Spirit-led, Spirit-empowered life.

Here she gives us a glimpse of the journey she has taken and shares a few life-giving practices she has adopted along the way.

Frontiers – Kathleen Doyle

Kathleen Doyle served as a pastor of Vintage Church Los Angeles in Santa Monica, California.

> But Jesus realizes that the most restful gift he can give the tired is a new way to carry life, a fresh way to carry responsibilities. . . . Realism sees that life is a succession of burdens; We cannot get away from them; Thus instead of offering escape, Jesus offers equipment. Jesus means that obedience to his sermon on the Mount [his yoke] will develop in us a balance and a "way" of carrying life that will give more rest than the way we have been living.[20]

Between 2007 and 2011, I had the privilege of watching the Holy Spirit lead a group of fearful, resistant believers (myself included) into a dynamic experience of God's healing and restorative presence. My involvement was a sheer act of mercy on God's part. I was afraid of the Holy Spirit, so it was absolutely ironic that I was charged with leading our church's prayer gatherings.

But let me back up and start from the beginning.

In 2007 I found myself in ministry and burning out. I had been a pastoral care staff member at two Southern California megachurches. I loved my work in many ways, but after a decade of hospital visits, support groups, leading and training volunteers, and counseling people in their deepest crises, I was fried. Even more challenging were the relational politics, isolation, and crushing expectations most ministers seem to experience. I was disillusioned and emotionally and spiritually spent, and I questioned how Jesus' promised "abundant life" factored into ministry life.

In the background of all the church activity was my personal life, which was not in the best shape. The Lord had nudged me to deal with some spiritual doubts and painful relationships, but I ignored the nudge and kept working. I hoped I could plow through until those issues somehow simply disappeared. Since I had surrounded myself with people who generally thought and acted like me, my approach seemed to make sense.

Though I didn't realize it then, I now know some of my burnout stemmed from my poor relationship with the Holy Spirit. To be honest, I was uncomfortable with him and kept him on the sideline of my spiritual life. I preferred reading my Bible and attempting to apply biblical principles, which felt more straightforward and less complicated than anything Holy Spirit-related.

My resistance to the Holy Spirit had deep roots.

In the late '80s and early '90s, a number of scandals erupted across several churches and high-profile ministries in the United States. The scandals were public and months-long investigative reports detailed stories of financial corruption, emotional manipulation, and sexual impropriety. Unfortunately, these incidents were primarily connected to "charismatic" and "Spirit-filled" churches and organizations.

I was a new believer at the time and had a lot to sort through, so I decided I would avoid anything "charismatic," emotional, or overtly "supernatural." In fact, I did my graduate work in pastoral care at a university considered "cessationist" regarding the work of the Holy Spirit. I moved forward in my faith, believing the Holy Spirit needed to be acknowledged but kept in check.

Back to 2007. As I slogged through the beginning stages of ministry burnout, a small group of wonderful people from England came to work with my team. They were unfamiliar with my brand of do-more-and-strategize-better-for-the-days-are-evil Christianity.

My new teammates were joy-filled, enthusiastic believers who regularly insulted me in the most loving way. For months, they asked me polite but pointed questions about my relationship with the Holy Spirit and continually pushed me to "be filled." To which I responded, "I am!"

I took my spiritual life seriously. I read my Bible daily. I was engaged in discipleship and spiritual disciplines. Yet I was tired, stressed, and disillusioned with the church. My soul felt heavy.

My British friends prodded to see if I had experienced a profound sense of God's love through the power of the Holy Spirit. They saw I was missing something important in my spiritual life.

During my time in seminary, I had taken a few courses on the spiritual disciplines. I read most of the books written by authors such as Richard Foster and Dallas Willard and had become familiar with the works of Saint Augustine, Catherine of Siena, and Bernard of Clairvaux. All are brilliant works from amazing believers I deeply respect, but I failed to understand these exercises needed to be done in the power of the Holy Spirit. I mistook reading and regular habits for intimacy. Without the life-giving power of the Holy Spirit, I associated the spiritual disciplines of silence, solitude, fasting, and simplicity with deep self-reflection and emotional isolation and exhaustion.

I had memorized but not experienced the reality of Ephesians 3:16–19:

> I pray that out of his glorious riches he may strengthen you with power through his Spirit in your inner being, so that Christ may dwell in your hearts through faith. And I pray that you, being rooted and established in love, may have power, together with all the Lord's holy people, to grasp how wide and long and high and deep is the love of Christ, and to know this love that surpasses knowledge—that you may be filled to the measure of all the fullness of God.

I didn't fully understand God's love. According to this passage, it's a love that surpasses understanding and provides strength for us. I had no idea how drained I was without it. I certainly didn't understand there was no chance I would ever know this incomprehensible love without the presence of the Holy Spirit.

At this time, my experience and expectations of the Holy Spirit comprised a few miraculous ministry experiences and occasional moments of feeling really, really guilty. I thought the Holy Spirit's role was to help me get stuff done. I had no idea part of his work was to reveal God's love to me.

I needed to take a fresh look at God's Word, believing Jesus meant what he said when he said his burden was light. I needed to reexamine some passages I had glossed over:

> And I will ask the Father, and he will give you another Helper, to be with you forever, even the Spirit of truth. (John 14:16–17, ESV)

If you then, though you are evil, know how to give good gifts to your children, how much more will your Father in heaven give the Holy Spirit to those who ask him! (Luke 11:13 ESV)

Very truly I tell you, whoever believes in me will do the works I have been doing, and they will do even greater things than these, because I am going to the Father. And I will do whatever you ask in my name, so that the Father may be glorified in the Son. You may ask me for anything in my name, and I will do it. (John 14:12–14)

These passages, along with several others and the entire book of Acts, challenged me to reconsider my damaged view of the Holy Spirit. As I studied, I prayed, "Lord, open my eyes and my ears." I wanted to see what I had been missing.

From these passages, I turned to the prayers of Paul and Jesus and began to make them my own. I read them slowly and repeatedly and prayed them out loud. By this time I knew part of the work of the Holy Spirit is to reveal who God is and his great love for us. But I had never actually sat still and personally asked the Holy Spirit to reveal these truths and promises to me.

When I finally did, he responded by asking me to make a few changes. I needed to slow down, revisit the practice of silence, and simplify my life. Like Jesus, I needed to see the value in *being with* God, not just *doing for* God.

Ironically, this stressed me out. Losing my packed schedule felt like losing my phone. How would I survive? My distractions kept me safe. It was one thing for the Holy Spirit to show me who God is; it was an entirely different story for him to tell me who I am.

I was also avoiding pain and emotional discomfort. If I kept busy and active, I didn't need to look at the doubts and stressors the Lord had been nudging me to address. And I didn't have to let go of the unhealthy control I was attempting to maintain over my life.

I was comfortable with ministry strategy, tasks, and study. But unlike administrative or intellectual interaction, engaging with the Holy Spirit felt vulnerable and personal. When it came to the Holy Spirit, I was allowing "someone else" to get involved, and I was unsure what he would bring up.

It was time to admit I was afraid. I was hiding from the Holy Spirit. I was afraid he would take over my life and/or me in some weird way. I was also fearful of experiencing the power of God in intimate and personal ways.

The first time I spent extended time waiting and listening for the Holy Spirit, I felt extremely vulnerable. What if he didn't say anything? What if he didn't want to speak to me? What if my faith was a fraud? What if He said something I didn't want to hear? Then I would be responsible and couldn't claim ignorance. What if my Holy Spirit experience was a figment of my imagination or the hype of a group gathering?

I also felt angry. I had a lot to do and sitting there in silence reminded me how irritated and frustrated I felt. What I had yet to learn was that those irritations and frustrations were exactly what I needed to bring to the Lord.

For most of my life, my prayers had been aimed in other directions. They were detached, compartmentalized. I wasn't speaking from my heart or having a genuine interaction with God. I was just reciting to him my list of concerns.

One day I clearly heard the Holy Spirit say, "Put the books down and go outside. All creation declares God's glory." So I went out on my balcony and stared at a tree—for far longer than I'd ever stared at a tree. I didn't realize it then, but I was being invited into biblical meditation. After that, I began to look more closely at creation and ask the Holy Spirit to open my eyes and ears so I might understand how it revealed God's nature.

I found myself continually prompted to ask God, "Who are you? What are you like?" Because I was paying more attention to his work,

I discovered that what is true of every artist is also true of God: an artist's creation always tells you something about the artist. I began to notice he was incredibly creative, he was funny, he was powerful, and he was beautiful.

The Holy Spirit was opening my eyes to see things about God I had never noticed or considered. Rather than experiencing silence and solitude as draining, the Holy Spirit's presence made me feel alive. Seeing God as creator was helping me see not just his power but also his personality, and I found him to be exciting and deeply enjoyable. The Psalms and other poetic passages carried a new weight and became so much more interesting. Seeing God in light of his dynamic nature began to change me. I was lighter. I had more joy. I felt more hope.

Author and pastor Sam Storms observes,

> We become like that which we behold. We will never be transformed into the likeness of God or be conformed to the image of Christ Jesus until we learn how to behold His beauty. To see Him is to be like Him. As David beheld the beauty of the Lord, as he meditated on the glorious perfections and passions of God's character, he became more like God. More than that, he fell ever more in love with God.[21]

What my British friends knew and what I was growing in is that the power of the Holy Spirit brings life, unity, courage, and strength.

Unexpectedly, I was asked to lead our church's weekly prayer night that had a small amount of momentum but was by no means vibrant. I was reluctant, to put it mildly. Though my own prayer life was rich, I had no experience in leading large group gatherings.

The only thing I knew to do was start where I had started. The only strategy we had was to gather, praise God in song, and pray to understand God. That was it.

Together, our small gathering began to pray the prayers of Paul and Jesus. Sometimes we sat in silence and waited for his presence to come. Sometimes we read a passage of Scripture slowly and asked the Lord to reveal himself. Sometimes we placed our hands on people and prayed God's presence and encouragement over them.

We asked the Lord to show us who he is, show us what he's like, and bring his love into our community. We didn't ask for healing. We didn't ask for the miraculous. We just asked for God. And as we asked for God, we saw healing and the miraculous occur.

We experienced the natural and loving way God moves among his people when his presence is welcomed and invited. I've never experienced God's presence and work more powerfully among a group of people.

REFLECTION QUESTIONS

1. Our mature walk with God is developed through daily surrender to him. In what new ways could you invite him into your daily life? To move from being a *consumer of* his grace to being a *participant with* his grace daily?

2. Our old identities were formed through environment and repetition, through time poured into them. What small decisions could you begin to make today to become an active participant in the formation of your new identity?

3. To his followers, Jesus was known for his prayer life, for his pursuit of "alone time" with his Father, for his unhurried pace, for the simplicity of his lifestyle. When you reflect on your own disciplines as a believer, which of these are a priority? Which disciplines need attention?

4. As a leader in a season of uncertainty, are you feeling disillusioned with God, the church, church leadership, relationships? In what areas are you fighting to keep your head above water? In your life and ministry are you experiencing the "light burden" and "abundant life" that Jesus promised?

5. Examine the fears Kathleen shared from her first extended time waiting and listening for the Holy Spirit. Do any of these resonate with you?

   - What if he didn't say anything?
   - What if he didn't want to speak to me?
   - What if my faith was a fraud?
   - What if he said something I didn't want to hear?
   - What if my Holy Spirit experience was a figment of my imagination or the hype of a group gathering?

3

EMPOWERED CULTURE

Foundation – Josh Harrison

. . . .

A few years ago, I was in West Jerusalem eating Sabbath dinner with a Jewish family. As we enjoyed the meal together, we got to talking about the land of Israel (*Eretz Yisrael*) and its significance in the lives of Jewish people. We talked about how it wasn't easy living in Israel, but my hosts (and countless other devout Jews) chose to stay because it was the only place they could truly be themselves. One of them explained to me, "There are 613 *mitzvot* (commandments) in the Torah, and until we returned to *Eretz Yisrael* (the land of Israel), we couldn't obey all of them. There are nearly thirty *mitzvot* that only apply to, and therefore can only be obeyed, in this land. Without this place, we cannot be and do everything God has commanded us."[22]

I've thought about this conversation often, both as it applies to the Jewish people and the nation of Israel and as it applies to myself as a Christian and a citizen of the kingdom of God. I've been to the Holy Land several times now, and honestly, I don't feel much connection to the place. Its people and their stories compel me, but even though my faith too was born there and my King walked that country, I don't share my Jewish friend's sense of intimacy with and obligation to that land. I've come to realize this is by design.

Unlike Judaism, the Christian faith is not tied to a place. In fact, throughout Jesus' life, he consistently undermined the idea of a holy land and place. Ultimately, he upended the traditional Jewish sense of mission and salvation by sending his followers to the nations rather than anticipating a great pilgrimage of the nations flocking to Israel for salvation.

For Jesus and for his church, there is no Holy Land. There is, instead, a holy people. And in the last conversation he had with his followers before he was crucified, Jesus gave them a *mitzvah* that could be accomplished only within the context of this holy people:

> A new command I give you: Love one another. As I have loved you, so you must love one another. By this everyone will know that you are my disciples, if you love one another. (John 13:34–35)

This command to show one another—and thereby the world—the radical, sacrificial, Spirit-empowered love of Jesus can only be obeyed in community. This means life with the Holy Spirit is not and must never be a solo venture. So far, we have spoken a lot about the personal aspects of our relationship with him, and while all of it is true and necessary, it's not the whole story.

The Holy Spirit did not come simply to empower a bunch of individuals into personal relationship with him but also into relationship with one another. He came to empower us into community in and through which he intends to demonstrate his love and power to the whole world.

He adopts us into a family, and we need one another to be ourselves, to do what Jesus has commanded us, and to experience the fullness of God's presence among us. We cannot live fully empowered lives apart from a local community of Spirit-filled Jesus followers. In other words, just as we must choose relationship with the Holy Spirit, we must also choose relationship with one another.

The early church modeled this beautifully. In Acts 2, immediately after the Holy Spirit came on the day of Pentecost and the church grew explosively overnight, they did this:

> They devoted themselves to the apostles' teaching and to fellowship, to the breaking of bread and to prayer. Everyone was filled with awe at the many wonders and signs performed by the apostles. All the believers were together and had everything in common. They sold property and possessions to give to anyone who had need. Every day they continued to meet together in the temple courts. They broke bread in their homes and ate together with glad and sincere hearts, praising God and enjoying the favor of all the people. And the Lord added to their number daily those who were being saved. (Acts 2:42–47)

This early group of disciples gave us a paradigm for how empowered life in the Spirit is supposed to work:

- When the Holy Spirit comes and fills individuals, they immediately cluster together so the love and power he gives each of them can be expressed, encouraged, and expanded in and through the community.
- The adopting Spirit of God draws people not only into relationship with their Father but also with their new sisters and brothers.
- In this new family, they begin to work out the implications of their new identities with one another.
- They not only each nurture their own relationship with God, but they also collectively develop a common life in the Spirit based on shared values and practices.

In summary, empowered people come together to form an empowered community that embodies an empowered culture to one another and the world.

The verb Luke uses in Acts 2 to describe the action of the early church is an important one. He says, "They *devoted* themselves." This is not a casual word used to describe loose affiliation or spontaneous acquaintance. These first Spirit-filled, Jesus followers were radically committed to this empowered life and community even to the exclusion of other priorities.

Dictionary definitions of the Greek word translated "devoted" are telling:

- "to persist obstinately" in a course of action[23]
- "to hold fast to, endure in, stand perpetually ready, persevere in"[24]
- "to continue to do something with intense effort, with the possible implication of despite difficulty"[25]

In other words, these first believers made a deliberate choice and significant effort to be and stay in community with one another. They made a costly commitment to each other and shared life in the Spirit.

The same must be true for us. Just as the Holy Spirit will not force us to be or grow in relationship with him, he also will not force us into relationship with one another. If we want to experience the fullness of his presence and the empowered life he has come to give us, we must devote ourselves to his church. We must persistently choose one another, even when faced with inconvenience or difficulty.

Empowered community is about much more than showing up once a week (or every other week) to a worship service where we sing songs about the Holy Spirit, where we pray, *"Come, Holy Spirit,"* where we pray for one another, and even where we exercise the gifts of the Spirit. It's about a lot more than a day. It is about lifelong devotion to this family into which he has adopted us.

This devotion in the early church is all the more significant when we consider the makeup of their community. The beginning of Acts 2 tells us this was an ethnically/culturally diverse group, with new members coming from "every nation under heaven" (Acts 2:5).

Further, we see throughout the book of Acts (as well as the Epistles) that this church was economically diverse, with rich and poor mingling together in community and even sharing meals. This may not seem especially significant to us, but in the ancient Roman world, the caste system was rigidly defined and maintained. Rich and poor rarely associated with one another and never did so on equal terms. This socioeconomic diversity would have been one of the most radical and compelling (or off-putting, depending on one's perspective) features of the early church.

Finally, and perhaps most significantly, this community was made up of people who until very recently had been at odds with one another. Remember, Peter's Pentecost sermon included a call to repentance for people who were complicit in the killing of Jesus. This was not merely metaphorical or spiritual language. Peter preached this sermon in the city where Jesus was crucified less than two months after it had happened. People who participated in Jesus' crucifixion were listening that day. People who participated in Jesus' crucifixion were baptized into the church that day. The disciples of Jesus, his closest followers and friends, were suddenly and unexpectedly in community with people who had killed him.

This was an unlikely an inconvenient community to which they devoted themselves. With every imaginable kind of diversity represented—even before the inclusion of Gentiles later in the book of Acts—this was not a community constructed for comfort. The Holy Spirit chose people the same way Jesus did: not for compatibility but for impact, not for ease but for transformation.

Nothing is especially compelling about a homogenous church. You can find that sort of community anywhere. Jesus' desire that the world see him by the ways we love one another will not happen if we choose community based on our own comfort and preference.

Instead, Jesus chooses and the Holy Spirit empowers people not for their similarities but for their differences—so that their sacrificial, inconvenient love for each other, empowered by the Spirit of love living within and among them, will be a powerful testimony of his love for the world. If we want to see the Holy Spirit move in powerful ways in and throughout our community, we must be serious about pursuing communities that are radically diverse and devoting ourselves to a church based not on its compatibility with our already-held preferences and opinions but on its potential for transformation—ours and the world around us.

The Bible calls this diverse community the "body of Christ."[26]

Now to each one the manifestation of the Spirit is given for the common good. To one there is given through the Spirit a message of wisdom, to another a message of knowledge by means of the same Spirit, to another faith by the same Spirit, to another gifts of healing by that one Spirit, to another miraculous powers, to another prophecy, to another distinguishing between spirits, to another speaking in different kinds of tongues, and to still another the interpretation of tongues. All these are the work of one and the same Spirit, and he distributes them to each one, just as he determines. Just as a body, though one, has many parts, but all its many parts form one body, so it is with Christ. For we were all baptized by one Spirit so as to form one body—whether Jews or Gentiles, slave or free—and we were all given the one Spirit to drink. Even so the body is not made up of one part but of many. (1 Corinthians 12:7–14)

For centuries these "gifts of the Spirit" (literally "spirituals" in Greek) have been the object of much study, discussion, and argument: how many gifts there are, how we identify who has which gifts, whether all gifts are still active, etc. But let's not get so bogged down in making lists and trying to fit ourselves and others into categories that we miss the big picture.

What Paul is telling us here is the Holy Spirit loves variety. He is the most powerful and creative person in the universe. And when his power and creativity interact with our own unique personalities joined in community, the result is a mosaic of temperaments, gifts, and resources empowered by the Holy Spirit for the sake of one another and the world. In another of his letters, Paul described this beautiful, diverse, compelling, wildly inconvenient community like this:

> Consequently, you are no longer foreigners and strangers, but fellow citizens with God's people and also members of his household, built on the foundation of the apostles and prophets, with Christ Jesus himself as the chief cornerstone. In him the whole building is joined together and rises to become a holy temple in the Lord. And in him you too are being built together to become a dwelling in which God lives by his Spirit. (Ephesians 2:19–22)

For the body of Christ to work properly, all sorts of different people need to play their parts. This requires something from both the people who call our churches "home" and the leaders God has entrusted with the care and stewardship of his churches.

From the people, there must be a commitment to community and a devotion to one another that goes beyond weekly attendance. We must all show up ready to offer what we have (what the Holy Spirit gives us) to the community. Church is not a spectator sport; for our communities to function the way God intends, everyone must play.

A pastor friend of mine tells a great story about a potluck she decided to host for the young adults in her church. She created a sign-up sheet, and everyone signed up to bring something delicious to share. When the day of the great feast finally arrived, everyone showed up eager to dig in—only to discover no one had signed up to bring forks. Rather than bail them out by running to the store, my friend decided to seize the opportunity to illustrate a point. "Well then, I guess we're just going to have to eat with our hands."[27]

You see, this is how it works in the body of Christ. If one of us, empowered by God to play a certain role in the body, doesn't play our part, then the whole body misses out and so does the world. A church is only as capable as its people are available.

As leaders, if we want to see this "everyone plays" culture thriving in our churches, we must create an environment where this is possible. This requires us to do three things:

First, we must create a robust church culture that extends beyond weekend gatherings. Many times, I've preached about the body of Christ and begged everyone to play their God-given part in our community, only to be convicted by the fact that I hadn't created space or imagination for them to do so. The truth is, we don't need a whole lot of people or gifts to pull off a weekend gathering. Even in very large churches, the volunteers needed to make a service happen likely represent a small percentage of the church community and an even smaller percentage of the gifts the Holy Spirit has lavished on the people in it.

In order to activate our whole community (the goal is always 100 percent), we have to expand our notion of what church is. Some of this will look like programmatic changes. We can add a groups ministry, start a non-profit, or look for other creative ways for people to engage and use their gifts. But much more will need to take place "outside" the organization as we broaden our horizons of "church."

If church is not a gathering, a building, a non-profit, or a set of ministries, but is instead a people, then most of the ministry the church does should happen outside the walls of the church in the daily lives of its people. In order for pastors and leaders to empower this kind of work, something else needs to happen.

Namely, leaders must know their people—not simply as attendees, but as people. Pastors and church leaders must take the call to pastoral care seriously and not only when people are in crisis. We need to "do life" with our people: know them, know their families, know their jobs, walk with them, eat with them, weep with them, celebrate with them. Pastors, our job is to be actively attentive to the presence and work of the Holy Spirit in the lives of our people so we can partner with him in that work. To do this, we must be in a relationship. We cannot empower people we don't know.

Finally, one of the most significant ways we can identify gifts and empower people is by creating cultures of prayer in our churches. We need to learn to hear from God on behalf of each other.

It is true that each of us has a relationship with the Holy Spirit who walks with us, lives in us, and advocates to us for us. But in the press of life, it is easy for us to lose sight of him. All the noise around (and within) us makes it difficult for us to hear his voice for ourselves. So God, in his grace, has invited us into community with others who also walk with him and hear from him. And when we are as committed to one another's growth in relationship with the Holy Spirit as we are to our own, he can use us to speak identity, power, and purpose into each other's lives.

In my church and many other churches, we call this "prayer ministry," and we try to make space for it every time we gather, whether in a weekend service, a staff meeting, a small group, or around a dinner table.

Creating this kind of prayer ministry culture is not easy. It requires intentionality (we regularly train our people to listen for the voice of the Holy Spirit and communicate what they are hearing humbly and lovingly) and commitment (there is always something else vying for our time). But there are few things that will have as great an impact on our communities and will go further toward creating the empowered culture we so long to see.

Bridge – Todd Proctor

Looking at these cultural distinctives that marked the early church, it's clear that what's desperately needed are compelling showcases of what empowered culture looks like here and now. As someone who is naturally wired for vision and strategy, I have slowly awakened over the years to realize culture really is the end zone. Vision is where you're going . . . but culture is who you become.

When a community truly becomes marked by a posture of Spirit-led expectancy, it's game-changing. I've seen this on display in many contexts around the world, but one of the most vibrant examples is very close to home.

Garden Church in Long Beach was planted out of a church I pastored in Orange County, California. A young couple, Darren and Alex Rouanzoin, were equipped and sent out to birth a new faith community in one of the most diverse and challenging cities in the nation. Subsequently, as seeds of prayer and sacrifice were sown into this new story, what began to break through the surface was marked by passionate partnership with the Holy Spirit.

Empowered culture wasn't just aspirational. It was undeniable.

Now a decade into the journey of pioneering Garden, my friend Darren shares some of his discoveries about how to cultivate a culture of Spirit-fueled "more" in your team and church.

Frontiers – Darren Rouanzoin

Darren Rouanzoin is the planter and lead pastor of Garden Church in Long Beach, California.

In 2015, a UPS driver walked into our church's office to deliver a package. At the time, our office was a 500-square-foot retail space with desks and couches juxtaposed like jigsaw pieces placed inches apart. The driver spotted me from the entrance and shouted, "Darren! I've been looking for you! I'm healed! Your prayer healed me!"

Caught off guard by the statement and the dramatic nature of the moment, my mind raced to catch up. While I was still forming a response, the driver went on to say, "I went back to church. I'm reading my Bible, and I can't even believe it!"

To this day, this simple sixty-second story amazes me. I'd like to tell you how and why.

I grew up in a church that didn't practice the "things of the Spirit." It was a traditional evangelical church that unintentionally taught me to worship the Father, the Son . . . and the Holy Bible. I eventually worked my way to a theology that was open to the Holy Spirit, but I wasn't a part of a church context that talked about the Spirit (except for convicting us of sin) or practiced the gifts of the Spirit in a worshiping community.

So when I got hired at a megachurch and traveled through London en route to a mission trip to India, I was shocked to find a church in the heart of central London that was reaching its city in the power of the Holy Spirit.

As a twenty-two-year-old rookie pastor, I sat raptly listening to the stories of this church. These weren't stories from decades past. They were new, fresh, last-week and yesterday stories: strangers prophesying and speaking knowledge in the workplace, men and women choosing to become Christian and leave other faiths and atheism. It was the stuff of the Bible, and it was happening every day in this church.

To my American ears, this was amazing, rare, exceptional! But to those telling the stories, it was normal. They absolutely celebrated and praised God for it, but they also expected it and weren't surprised when it happened on a regular basis. I had never experienced anything like it, and I was hungry for more.

Eventually, one pastor extended an invitation: "Why don't we all stand up and pray for each other?" So we all did. And I was forever changed. Someone prayed for me, and I felt a rush of energy in my body. God ambushed me in a way that was tangible and real. I encountered the Holy Spirit in ways I had never experienced before. I wept. I was filled with peace, joy, and a sense of purpose. Even more, I had a deeper desire for intimacy with God.

That day changed me. I knew God's Spirit was real and alive, and the Holy Spirit was operating within and through the church just like we read in the Scriptures. From then on, I knew I wanted to pursue the presence of God. The only problem was I hadn't been a part of a church that created space or raised disciples to depend on God's presence for the life of the church. Instead, we were taught how to use programs, strategy, theory, talent, and proficiencies to help build larger churches and get people into seats. No one had taught me how to expect and depend on the Holy Spirit.

I believe this is one of the greatest failures of the modern church. If we are going to raise up the next generation and reach a changing world, we must create space in every area of our churches for the Holy Spirit to move, minister, and lead. We need to create an empowered culture. This is not about a strategy, program, or class; it is a way of living and leading communities. This is about a way of being that is permeated with the reality of God's presence with us, for us, and empowering us to do the things Jesus did in the New Testament here and now!

Shortly after my experience in London with the Holy Spirit, I heard the Lord speak to me as clear as day. He said, "Plant a church in Long Beach." One year later, my wife, Alex, and I started a church in downtown Long Beach, California. For the past eleven years, we've had the privilege of helping build a ministry dependent on the Holy Spirit and thriving as an empowered culture.

It's been an exhilarating adventure with a steep learning curve and rich rewards. To help you on your journey, I want to share five practical steps we've learned about building and contending for empowered church culture.

1. *What you build within you will be built around you.* There is no way around this one. If you want to build a church dependent upon the ministry of the Holy Spirit, you must cultivate a life in the Spirit. This is how culture is built. You can't delegate, hire, or create a committee to make this happen for you. It must be built into, practiced in, and shared in your life. You cannot replicate something that's not in you.

I remember spending a few days with a prominent leader in Northern California whose globally influential church is known for the ministry and power of the Holy Spirit. After following this pastor around for a few days, I asked him, "How do I create this kind of culture at my church? What do I do?"

I was looking for a tried-and-true formula that produces the kind of culture and outcomes his church was experiencing. He paused, looked me in the eye, and asked me, "Do you really want this for your church?"

"Absolutely!" I replied energetically, pen and paper in hand.

He said, "Okay. Go home, and the next time you are having a meal with your family, look at your six- and three-year-old. Ask them this simple question: 'If Jesus walked into the room right now, what would he say to Mommy?'" He looked at me and smiled. "What you build within you will be built around you. And this culture you desire starts with your life and your family. They cannot be separated!"

I was looking for strategy, a class, a sermon, a book, or a sermon series. The pastor had given me something far more compelling: a life.

The simple truth is you must build whatever you are hoping for within the church into your life first. You must stay hungry for God's presence. You must practice and mature in the things of the Spirit. Only then will it emerge around you naturally.

2. *A church within the church.* Whatever you want the whole church to experience, your leadership teams need to experience first.

When we started pursuing the Holy Spirit, we began with our leaders. We began teaching through the book of Acts and creating space for the Holy Spirit in our staff and elder meetings. This space quickly became a learning community for the ministry of the Holy Spirit. We didn't strategize the Holy Spirit; we invited and waited for him.

This meant creating a mini-church service for our staff and elder meetings. It meant worshiping, laying hands, prophesying, practicing words of knowledge with each other, and anticipating God to heal and do all the beautiful things that accompany the ministry of the Spirit. At first, it felt unnatural and uncomfortable. But building culture requires repetition and practice. We kept meeting, praying, seeking, and waiting for God, and he showed up in our midst and ministered to us.

As a result, our culture began to shift. Every meeting began with prayer and the anticipation that God wanted to speak and we could and would hear his voice. Staff meetings became powerful God encounters. Elder meetings became a place for intercession and crying out to God. Leader gatherings became a facilitation of the ministry and power of the Holy Spirit. It seemed as if every meeting was hijacked by God's power and presence and we had to learn to respond to his voice and guidance—to hear and obey.

This intentionality moved into every area of ministry. By the time the ministry of the Holy Spirit showed up in our weekend gatherings, it was already taking place everywhere else. This is what I mean by a church within a church.

Take your leaders on this journey. Make time to worship and pray for one another in your staff and leadership meetings. Use the space to encounter God and build the culture you want to see throughout your whole church community.

3. *Celebrate the stories.* Over the years, I've learned nothing builds culture faster than the stories you celebrate. We started celebrating stories of the Spirit moving in our church by sharing what we call "good news stories" in every staff and leadership meeting. We asked every staff member or leader to bring firsthand, personally

experienced stories that were fresh (within the past week) and celebrated the hope we had for the church to encounter God.

These were stories of generosity, risk, both successes and failures, and they were small and big examples of the kind of church we were working to become. We celebrated obedience, not just outcomes.

Our storytelling started small and was awkward at first, but we kept at it. As a joke, I started telling the staff if they didn't have a story to share, they couldn't attend the meeting. So some weeks, an hour before our meeting, staff would go out and pray for people on the streets. As a result, strangers accepted Jesus as their Lord and Savior and joined Alpha or a community group. This is the power of taking risks, expecting God to move, and telling the stories.

Practically, you can implement this immediately. Encourage each staff member to bring a "good news story" every week. Not every week will include a miracle report, but every week there will be stories of risk and intentionality toward becoming the kind of church that sees the Holy Spirit move.

4. *Faith is spelled R-I-S-K.* Faith is required for our journey and maturity as Christians. Whatever faith was for you yesterday is not going to be faith for you tomorrow. Faith is not supposed to remain perpetually the same but is supposed to grow. The only way to grow is by reaching beyond what you know, have experienced, and can do.

Specifically, to build a church culture dependent on the Holy Spirit, collectively you have to put yourself in a position where you need and invite him to do his work. Only when we dare to step into that uncomfortable space of trusting God to move will we see that he can, does, and will. This is why we pray for strangers, ask for healing, invite people to Alpha, and the list goes on. Without risk, you leave no room for the Spirit to work. Risk is essential.

By the time I met the UPS driver whom I mentioned earlier, I had shared with my teams and congregation dozens and dozens of stories of my attempts—risks—to invite God's healing power on behalf of someone who needed it. So far, I didn't know of any of my prayers that had been answered with healing. But I wanted to see God move, and I continued to believe he would.

When the UPS driver knocked on my door the first time I met him, he had braces around both knees and long, black wraps around both elbows. I asked him what happened and if he was in pain. He said, "Yes, it's bad, and I'm about to go on disability because I can't do this job anymore."

I asked him, "Can I pray for you?"

He said, "Sure."

So with very little faith, because I had prayed this same prayer dozens of times before with seemingly no response, I put my hand on his shoulder and said, "Lord Jesus, heal my brother. Amen!" That was it. I grabbed my package and closed the door as soon as I could because I was embarrassed and didn't think anything would really happen. He walked away.

A month later, he walked into my office and filled the crowded space with the news of what God had done. It was undeniable. This UPS driver went from near disability to complete healing. A few years later I saw him driving his truck. He pulled over to tell me how much his had life changed because of that prayer. Isn't that funny? This man's whole life changed because of a half-hearted, faith-deficient, done-out-of-obedience prayer.

5. *Pray, pray, pray.* The number-one way to create an empowered culture is to pray for it. Prayer is the language of the Holy Spirit, and we must learn to speak his language. Prayer is the central role we must play as the shepherds of our flocks. Prayer must become an everyday, long-game strategy of building culture.

I (and countless others) have prayed long and hard for Garden Church to be a church where the Spirit of God is present, where the gifts of the Spirit are practiced and manifested, and where God's power is evident in all areas of ministry. In numerous ways, this prayer has become a living, thriving reality. And in faith, we humbly continue to pray for even more.

This is the purpose of our churches: to be empowered, refreshed, energized, and baptized in the presence of God for the sake of his mission in the world.

As you train your community to pursue God, he will meet you where you are and take it from there. You will see an increased expectancy of what's possible. You will see a hunger for God's presence in your gatherings. You will see God move you into new territories and places you've never imagined. You'll get to watch as followers of Jesus begin to live out their faith in incredible ways. And these "ways" happen to look very much like the stories in the New Testament that push the boundaries of the church into new frontiers. Which, I suppose, is the point. As Luke writes in Acts 1:8, "But you will receive power when the Holy Spirit comes on you; and you will be my witnesses in Jerusalem, and in all Judea and Samaria, and to the ends of the earth."

REFLECTION QUESTIONS

1. Josh shares that Jesus' command to love one another can only be obeyed in community—that we must choose relationships with one another. Do you find it difficult to make the effort to be in and stay in community regularly? Or are you eager to grab every opportunity to live in community with others? The need for authentic, Spirit-empowered community is as true for leaders as it is for those we are leading.

2. With every imaginable kind of diversity representing the body of Christ in Acts 2, consider your areas of leadership in your church, team, or network. Describe the diversity that exists in them. What is missing? What are the most significant factors limiting Acts 2 diversity in these areas?

3. What would an empowered, "everyone plays" culture look like in the body of Christ you've been entrusted to lead?

4. What you build within you will be built around you. You cannot replicate something that's not in you. What could you do to create more of an empowered culture in yourself?

5. How could you intentionally create more space for the ministry of the Holy Spirit in the communities or meetings you lead? What might get in your way?

4

EMPOWERED MISSION

Foundation - Josh Harrison

· ·

Back in chapter one, we learned the foundation of the empowered life is love. Out of the abundance of his love for us, the Father sent his Son, full of the Spirit, into the world so we might be restored to relationship with him, ourselves, one another, and the world around us. Having completed that work through his life, death, and resurrection, Jesus now sends the same Spirit by which he lived, died, and rose into each of his followers to be the ongoing presence of his love for us. This is who the Holy Spirit is, and this is what he is doing in our lives.

To be "empowered" is to live in relationship with God by his Spirit, to understand more and more who Jesus is and what he has done for us, to grow daily in the experiential knowledge of his endless love. Any conversation about the power of the Holy Spirit must begin here. But it must not end here. The empowering love of God given *to us* by the Holy Spirit must be given *through us* to the world. This is why he has adopted us, not simply so we can enjoy being his kids—though we can *and should*—but so we can join him in the work he is doing in the world.

This is how adoption worked in the first century. One did not adopt a child so they could choose their own path in life, but so they could be heirs of and partners in the family business. Adopted children of merchants became merchants. Adopted children of landowners became landowners. As we've already mentioned, in a few famous cases, the adopted children of emperors became emperors. In fact, they were adopted *so they could be the emperor.* This gift of adoption is not simply about new identity, but it's also about new vocation.

In the same way, our new identities as daughters and sons of God come with a job description. His love is for us—always for us, more-than-we-can-ever-fully-understand for us—but it is not just about us. It's so much bigger than that! God lavishes his love on us through the ongoing presence of his Holy Spirit *so that* through us, he can lavish his love on the whole world. He intends for us not only to be recipients but also conduits of his Spirit. Understanding this is essential to living the empowered life. He is not only the Spirit of adoption but also the Spirit of mission.

As in all things, Jesus shows us what this is supposed to look like. Let's start in Luke 3:

> When all the people were being baptized, Jesus was baptized too. And as he was praying, heaven was opened and the Holy Spirit descended on him in bodily form like a dove. And a voice came from heaven: "You are my Son, whom I love; with you I am well pleased." (Luke 3:21–22)

Jesus was not the adopted but the begotten Son of God. Nevertheless it was still vital for him to hear the voice of the Father affirm his identity and to receive the power and presence of the Holy Spirit as the sign and seal of that identity. And it's significant this encounter took place before Jesus launched his public life. Before Jesus ever did anything in ministry, his Father loved him and was pleased with him. He *was* before he *did*.

This is essential. This is why we started our conversation about the power of the Holy Spirit where we did. If we don't know who we are, we can never do what he's made us to do. Identity must always be our starting point, but again, as we'll see Luke 4, it is not our ending point. The work of the Holy Spirit doesn't stop there.

Immediately, after the Father and Spirit affirmed Jesus' identity as the beloved and well-pleasing Son of God, the same Spirit sent—and accompanied—him into the wilderness where this identity was tested: "If you are the Son of God" (Luke 4:3, 9). Jesus' identity was secure, but he still had to choose to *participate* with the Father and the Holy Spirit in that identity. After he passed the test—though I'm sure he, like us, had to pass similar tests most days of his life—Jesus returned from the wilderness, walked into a synagogue in his hometown, and this happened:

> He went to Nazareth, where he had been brought up, and on the Sabbath day he went into the synagogue, as was his custom. He stood up to read, and the scroll of the prophet Isaiah was handed to him. Unrolling it, he found the place where it is written: "The Spirit of the Lord is on me, because he has anointed me to proclaim good news to the poor. He has sent me to proclaim freedom for the prisoners and recovery of sight for the blind, to set the oppressed free, to proclaim the year of the Lord's favor." Then he rolled up the scroll, gave it back to the attendant and sat down. The eyes of everyone in the synagogue were fastened on him. He began by saying to them, "Today this scripture is fulfilled in your hearing." (Luke 4:16–21)

The Spirit of God was on him, he said, for a purpose. The power of the Holy Spirit was with him *so* he could participate in the mission of God in the world, *so* he could partner with his Father in the family business. This is what sons do.[28]

But Luke 4 doesn't stop there. Jesus didn't simply tell us the Holy Spirit empowered him for a purpose. He also told us exactly what that purpose is. He outlined for us the details of the mission. With the book of Isaiah as a reference point, Jesus described the family business as the proclamation of good news.

In our current-day context we have come to think of and use the term "gospel" almost exclusively in Christian settings. To most, it has become a "religious" word, but this was not the case in the ancient world.

The word "gospel" was used in the Roman Empire in non-religious contexts as well. One of the most famous examples comes from the time period immediately after Emperor Nero committed suicide without making provisions for a successor. For a year, the empire descended into chaos and turmoil as four men vied for control of Rome. Ultimately, a man named Vespasian secured the throne, established a new dynasty, and brought peace and stability to the empire. The ancient scholar Josephus described Vespasian's reign as "gospel"—good news that "the whole empire [was] now secured and the Roman state saved beyond expectation."[29]

This was the cultural context for the term "gospel" at the time of the writing of the New Testament. And this is exactly what Jesus had in mind when he used the word in Nazareth that day.

You see, the world's backstory is not all that different from the Roman Empire in AD 69. Through sin—original and ongoing—humans have forfeited and continue to forfeit the power God gave us to steward his creation in relationship with him in a way that reflects his character, his image, to the world. When we choose to settle for less than the relationship, identity, and purpose for which God created us, we abdicate our throne and hand our God-given power over to what the Bible refers to as "the powers." Paul describes them in his letter to the Ephesians as "the rulers, . . . the authorities, . . . the powers of this dark world and . . . the spiritual forces of evil in the heavenly realms."[30]

What do these powers do with the power we give them? They wield our own power and birthright to oppress and enslave us. They throw our lives and our world into turmoil and chaos, and we, rather than rule as God intended us to, now struggle to survive in the world the powers have made. We come up with all sorts of coping strategies and defense mechanisms, most of which involve not stewarding and shepherding, but using and abusing the world and one another in order to make ourselves feel more secure in our insecurity.

So when Jesus came into this broken world and announced the Good News that the kingdom of God has come near, he was proclaiming a regime change. Here was a new ruler who lived by the power of and in step with the Spirit of God—empowered and participating in his true identity and vocation. And he would break the endless cycle of oppression and restore the rest of us to our God-given identity and vocation.

The powers were trembling and would soon be defeated. The chaos, fear, and oppression that accompanied their reign was coming to an end. Hiding and coping were no longer needed. We could finally be free to claim our rightful place at his side and the head of creation. A new age of freedom and restoration had begun. Using the words of Isaiah, Jesus called this new age "the year of the Lord's favor," which is another way of saying "the Year of Jubilee."

Jubilee was a remarkable practice commanded by God in the book of Leviticus. According to Old Testament law, it was to take place every fifty years. During the year of Jubilee, three things were supposed to happen: slaves were to be freed, debts were to be canceled, and all land was to be returned to its original owners. In other words, it was a year of radical grace and restoration.

In his Nazareth synagogue proclamation, Jesus defined his purpose in precisely these terms. He came to announce and embody radical grace and restoration by the presence and power of the Holy Spirit. This is *why*, Jesus said, the Spirit was on him: so he could partner with his Father in this work of emancipation, restoration, and Jubilee. Jesus showed us in that moment and throughout the rest of his life how Spirit-empowered identity works itself out in mission.

The abundance of the Father's love for him overflowed to the world around him.

And he said the same must be true of us. Shortly after he rose from the dead, Jesus appeared to his disciples and did something remarkable:

> Again, Jesus said, "Peace be with you! As the Father has sent me, I am sending you." And with that he breathed on them and said, "Receive the Holy Spirit." (John 20:21–22)

This is startling. Everything that is true of him, Jesus said, is now true of us. Through his love and obedience, we are given his inheritance; we are adopted into his Sonship. This identity is affirmed and sealed through the Word of God and the presence of the Holy Spirit. We, like him, must choose to participate with the Holy Spirit in our identities. We must choose, through hardship and trial, to be and become who God says we already are. And he has done all of this for us *so* we can continue the mission he began, *so* we can partner with him in his work in the world, *so* we can take our place in the family business. In other words, he sends us into the world *in the same way the Father sent him*: with the same identity, empowered by the same Spirit, for the same purpose.

We must never separate our Spirit-empowered identities as beloved children of God from his mission in the world. His Spirit fills us and remains with us so we can be his children who partner with our Father in the family business. In fact, Scottish theologian Andrew Murray goes so far as to say, "No one may expect to be filled with the Spirit if he is not willing to be used for missions."[31] Of course, Murray is not saying we cannot receive the Holy Spirit in any way without a heart for mission; he is simply pointing out that growth in our relationship with the Holy Spirit should result in growth of our passion for mission. He is the missional Spirit of God sent to invite us into the Father's work in the world.

Jesus again made this connection between personal empowerment and missional movement clear in the moments before he ascended into heaven.

> But you will receive power when the Holy Spirit comes on you; and you will be my witnesses in Jerusalem, and in all Judea and Samaria, and to the ends of the earth. (Acts 1:8)

The power of the Holy Spirit would be given to his followers, Jesus said, so they could be witnesses, power for the sake of mission. And the disciples who were there that day took this call to mission seriously. They did as he instructed and went to Jerusalem to wait for this promised power.[32]

Their waiting was not passive. They were not simply biding their time, frittering away the hours until God showed up. They were active participants in the coming of the Holy Spirit. They gathered, according to Acts 1, for ten days in constant prayer. They knew they could not force him to show up, but they would be ready when he did. And, when he did, their private prayer gathering became a public spectacle.

They spilled out of the room where they had been gathered and into the streets of Jerusalem, all of them speaking "the wonders of God" in languages they had never spoken before.[33] When a crowd gathered to see what was going on, they did exactly what Jesus told them to do. They witnessed. More accurately, they became witnesses. They were no longer fishermen, housewives, businesspeople, tax collectors, and such. The Holy Spirit compelled them into and empowered them for a new vocation, a new purpose. They exchanged their plans, ambitions, and dreams for his. They adopted his mission as their own. They took their place in the family business.

As a result, the gospel of the kingdom spread across Jerusalem, Judea, and Samaria, and to the ends of the earth. Just like Jesus said it would.

This relationship between personal empowerment and missional movement has been present in every significant move of God throughout history. The work of the Spirit in a small Moravian community in Herrnhut in the 1700s resulted in the birth of the modern mission movement and the transformation of the world as we know it. We would not be here today were it not for that small group of Spirit-filled followers of Jesus. The Welsh revival, which was marked by powerful manifestations of the Holy Spirit, overflowed into mission both across Wales and around the world. At the Azusa Street revival in Los Angeles, there was famously a box where people who had received the gift of the Holy Spirit could give money to missionary work *or take money* as they were empowered for mission. Within two years so many missionaries had gone out from Azusa Street that the movement had spread to over fifty nations.

Great outpourings of the Holy Spirit always serve to ignite mission. True revival begins on a personal and local level but always reaches a global level as the Holy Spirit empowers and compels us out into the world to live as his children and partners in our family business.

A few years back, I had the opportunity to swim in both the Sea of Galilee and the Dead Sea within a twenty-four-hour period. The difference between the two experiences was striking. The Sea of Galilee was cool, clean, and refreshing: a wonderful place to spend a summer afternoon. The Dead Sea, on the other hand, was hot, smelly, and caustic. It was a fascinating but not altogether pleasant experience.

What's interesting is that both bodies of water are fed by the same Jordan River. Both experience the same fresh, clean water pouring in, but only the Sea of Galilee sends the water out as well. This is the key to keeping its water fresh and clean and making it a place that can sustain life. Where water comes in but doesn't flow out, it quickly becomes stale, stagnant, and uninhabitable. The same is true of our life with the Holy Spirit.

In John 7, Jesus famously said:

> Let anyone who is thirsty come to me and drink. Whoever
> believes in me, Scripture has said, rivers of living water will flow
> from within them. (John 7:37–38)

John went on to explain:

> By this he meant the Spirit, whom those who believed in him
> were later to receive. Up to that time the Spirit had not been
> given, since Jesus had not yet been glorified. (John 7:39)

Notice this relationship with the Holy Spirit, whom Jesus calls
"living water," consists of both an inlet—"If you're thirsty, come
and drink"—and an outlet—"out of you will flow rivers." Both are
essential for vibrant life in and relationship with the Holy Spirit.
When we view ourselves not as the destination of the Holy Spirit but
as channels through which he flows to a dry and weary world, we
not only participate with him in the work he is doing in the world,
but we also ensure our own relationships with him are always vibrant
and flourishing.

Adoption and mission are not only inseparable; they are also
symbiotic. They edify one another. Where adoption thrives, mission
follows; and where mission is prioritized, adopted identity is
reinforced and revitalized.

Participation in the mission of God is one of the primary ways
by which we maintain and grow intimacy with our Father. This is
the beauty and genius of the Holy Spirit: when we are truly filled
with his presence, power, and love, it overflows to the world. And as
it overflows to the world through us—as we make ourselves available
for his mission—we experience his presence, power, and love anew.

Identity inspires mission, and mission invigorates identity.
Knowing who we are, we go to work in the family business, and as

we work the family business, we grow in the knowledge of who our Father is and who we are.

Bridge - Todd Proctor

As Josh describes our adoptive birthright to be "partners in the family business," this invitation will lead some across the world to unreached nations. But for many more, it is just as critical to let a mission take you across a street, cubicle, or dining room table. With most of the Western world in deep post-Christian drift, the urgent need to showcase the love of Jesus has never hit closer to home. The Great Commission calls us not only to communist strongholds or hostile tribal chiefs but soccer moms and Starbucks baristas. And it seems for most Jesus followers, the call to be a "witness" can be intimidating in any context.

My friend Craig Springer is one of those people who wakes up most days with the cry of the lost on his heart and mind. When he first discovered his destiny in Jesus in his twenties, he couldn't help but answer the call to get the word out to others. This passion led him to Prague as a church planter, and then to help pastor a megachurch renowned for its commitment to evangelism.

In recent years, Craig stepped in to take the helm of Alpha USA. Alpha is a tool birthed in London decades ago that has helped millions around the world take a journey of discovering Jesus. The hospitable space it creates for skeptics to bring questions, concerns, or even hostility about faith to the table has never seemed more needed than now. But anyone who has been a part of an Alpha course will tell you the true "secret sauce" is dependence on the Spirit.

As has often been said, these free-flowing, nothing's-off-limits dinner conversations seem designed to fail unless God shows up. And countless salvation stories now showcase the way he does.

Here, Craig brings us into a few of these moments as he recounts the way the Spirit empowers mission by filling ordinary people to welcome home spiritual orphans in extraordinary ways.

Frontiers – Craig Springer[34]

Craig Springer is the executive director of Alpha USA.

Not long ago, a man's wife invited him to church. The man (we'll call him Allen) didn't have much interest in spiritual matters. He was a logical thinker and considered religion to be largely emotional. But his wife kept inviting him, so he checked out the church online. *Well,* he thought, *they don't seem entirely crazy.* So he went.

That's when Allen heard about Alpha, and something about the straightforwardness of the content and format appealed to him. So he signed up and attended Alpha every week, participating in the conversations and categorizing everything he learned.

Every week he also asked the pastor, Jay, for additional resources—books, videos, articles, podcasts, etc. Allen surprised himself by how interested he was in the Christian faith and how much time he was spending on research.

All of this eventually led to Alpha's weekend away, when everyone spends some extended time together thinking deeply about God and being introduced to prayer and the Holy Spirit. Allen decided to go along, but he had some reservations.

Just before the opening talk of the weekend, Allen approached Jay. "I know what's going on," he said. And he proceeded to tell Jay he could tell the crescendo was coming, and he was going to be asked or manipulated to do something completely based on emotion.

"That's not true, Allen," Jay said. "There's no manipulation coming for you this weekend. And please don't do anything you don't want to do. That's not why we're here."

Allen looked skeptical.

"I'm serious," Jay said. "No shouting. We're not going to dim the lights or pull on your heartstrings. Nothing like that. We're just going to teach you about the Holy Spirit and give you a chance to pray."

"Okay," Allen said, but there was still doubt in his voice.

Later during the service, Jay talked about how to experience God's presence, and then extended an invitation. "If you want someone to pray with you, if you want to have an experience with God, stand up where you are, and one of us will come and pray with you."

Allen stood up.

"Why are you standing?" asked Jay, a little confused by their earlier conversation.

"I'm already here," Allen explained, shrugging. "If this stuff you're talking about is true, then it's worth trying."

Jay walked to where Allen was standing, put his hand on Allen's shoulder, and prayed quietly, "Allen, be filled with the Holy Spirit."

After a few moments of waiting, Allen doubled over and started weeping intensely. He cried and cried, completely overcome.

Later that day, Allen found Jay and pulled him aside. "Jay, this stuff is real."

Jay smiled. "Yeah, I know it is."

"No," Allen repeated. "This stuff is real, like gravity is real."

"Yeah," Jay said, laughing this time. "I know it's real. As real as gravity."

Something had shifted in Allen. He went from contemplating a philosophy to encountering a reality. Allen had given himself fully to Jesus and his heart and life began to change even more after that one experience.

He went from seeking an explanation about God to experiencing God. And his journey didn't stop there.

EXPLANATION EQUALS EXPERIENCE

I led evangelism and outreach efforts in two large churches. I also remember shaking my head at the results of those outreaches. Were those numbers correct?

Disappointingly, the results were much lower than any of us desired. Nothing we were doing was working particularly well. And no matter how confident we were, no matter how much money we spent, the results never lived up to our hopes.

Why weren't more people coming to know Jesus?

Why weren't those who came forward or raised their hands to follow Jesus coming back to church?

Was the transformation simply not sticking?

I was disappointed and frustrated. We strategized, worked hard, and executed the plans we created, but nothing was quite as fruitful as we hoped.

One day I read Romans 1:16 with fresh eyes, and my entire perspective shifted:

> For I am not ashamed of the gospel, because it is the power of God that brings salvation to everyone who believes.

Have you ever read a Bible verse you've read many times before, and suddenly it became saturated with new meaning? I reread this verse again and again.

If I'm being completely honest, I had been living, leading, and training others as if the gospel, the Good News, was the *explanation of man* for the salvation of those who believed. Or maybe I was living as if the gospel was *the strategy of the church and my efforts to be productive* for the salvation of those who believe.

But that's not what the verse says. It says the gospel "is the power of God that brings salvation to everyone who believes."

The power of God.

Here's the problem: I was acting as if the key was people knowing enough *about* the gospel, as if it could be fully understood and internalized through explanation alone.

I realized I needed to depend more on the power and the person of God.

Leading people into an experience with God himself is one of the bedrocks of Alpha. It is a process that allows people—through listening and conversation, belonging, building trust, and time—to strip away every barrier, arriving at a place where they can finally experience God for themselves.

That is what we are always trying to do: introduce people not just to a religion or system of beliefs, but into a *relationship* of experienced love, felt grace, and transforming power in the here and now.

In a recent study conducted by Alpha and Barna Group, one of the highest-ranked factors non-Christians said would increase their interest in faith was a personal "eye-opening spiritual experience."[35] People long for that. They long to feel a connection with the person who created them, has a purpose for them, and loves them.

The true power of evangelism comes from an introduction to the Holy Spirit of God, an invitation to his presence. The deep, spiritual hunger in our world today is for much more than an explanation; it is for a personal experience and a real relationship that can be counted on.

Jay Pathak, the pastor who led Allen into his experience of God through Alpha, is the lead pastor of five neighborhood churches just outside of Denver. In the last handful of years they have collectively baptized more than a thousand people, and they follow up with everyone who is baptized, begins a relationship with Jesus, or takes an Alpha course.

One interesting thing they've learned is that somewhere around 70 percent of those who decided to follow Jesus had some kind of supernatural experience that led them to make that decision.

"We've seen that in Alpha as well," says Jay. "The people who attend are thinking, processing, and opening their hearts to different ways of considering Jesus, and this helps them move beyond obstacles they've run into previously. Alpha gives them some space that's not hyped or contrived, where they can invite God to speak to them directly. And the number of people who have some kind of encounter with God is astounding."

If we want evangelism to revive, we must move away from relying on explanation alone, and extend invitations and create spaces for them to experience God.

What can we do to facilitate these kinds of life-changing encounters with God? Here are some ideas:[36]

Do you regularly have experiences with the living God? You can't take people to places you've never been. If we want to introduce our friends or fellow churchgoers to experiences with God, then we have to experience God ourselves. The kingdom is among us! We should all be experiencing the presence and power of the Spirit.

Where is God already at work? If you want to lead others toward experiencing God, it's important to stop and think about how God is already at work in you, through you, and around you, in the places you already are. Your job in facilitating experiences with God isn't to get people to do certain things or be a certain way. Your responsibility includes getting them to see what is already there.

One reason Alpha seems to be effective is the course leads people to take baby steps on their spiritual journey. With each step they're not looking for God in some far-off place but the world around them. Their conversations with other Alpha participants, their growing interest in the Bible, and learning to pay closer attention to others all help them begin to see they can experience God at any time through the people and events right in front of them.

Listen and pay attention. God is working, moving, and acting in you and where you are. Are you seeing it? Are you hearing his voice?

Paying attention might mean having a heart-to-heart conversation with (or simply listening to) your child or spouse. It might mean getting your neighbor's name and phone number. It might mean going to an AA meeting with your friend or calling a family member you haven't spoken to in a while. Listen to the places the Spirit within you is leading. Pay attention to the life going on around you.

Pray. Once you start listening and paying attention, prayer is the next logical step. Ultimately, experiencing God involves praying. If you believe praying is talking with (not just to) the God of the universe, then start praying about the places you are and the people who are with you. Above all, ask to see what God wants you to see.

Create space for God. At some point in the evangelistic process we have to say, "You may not get all these questions and doubts answered. But if God is real, he will show up. Why don't we ask God to show up and see what happens?"

This is a cliffhanger moment. We like to say, "Alpha is perfectly designed to fail unless God shows up." Because it *is* perfectly designed to fail. It's filled with explanation and conversation and belonging and radical hospitality, but we are ultimately waiting for the power of God alone to lead people to salvation.

Shouldn't this be true of all our evangelism efforts, that they are perfectly designed to fail unless God shows up? We must create physical and conversational space in our strategies and efforts, bringing people to that cliff's edge where God must show up. If not, all we have is a bunch of good human intentions.

Expect exponential impact. When we lead people into spaces where they can experience God, we aren't only unleashing the power of God in their lives. God will begin to move out from them to their friends, family, neighbors, colleagues, and classmates. It's like when a rock is tossed into the middle of a pond: the ripples spread outward, reaching to the furthest banks.

Remember Allen, who experienced God so deeply he gave his life to Jesus Christ? Now, he and his entire family bring their friends to church. After a recent teaching on giving, Allen decided he wanted to give more than the 10 percent that Scripture suggests.

Allen had been in church for months before that transforming moment at Alpha's weekend retreat. During those months he heard a lot of important and valuable explanations—about the Bible, about the church, and about God.

But it wasn't until he experienced God for himself that his life transformed. It was the experience of God that helped all the knowledge finally make sense, click into place, and put the ripple effect in motion.

Explanation is important. Logic and reason and learning about the truth are essential. But those efforts cannot stand on their own because the gospel is the power of God for the salvation of those who believe.

REFLECTION QUESTIONS

1. Jesus' identity was confirmed by God before his public ministry, and then his identity was tested. When have you felt your identity was tested? What is the Holy Spirit saying to you about your identity completely independent from your ministry?

2. Jesus offered a regime change of radical grace and restoration and gave it to us. How can you be the conduit of a "regime" change in your circle as Jesus was?

3. Consider the Sea of Galilee and Dead Sea illustration. The relationship with the Holy Spirit, whom Jesus called "living water," consists of both an inlet—"If you're thirsty, come and drink"—and an outlet—"out of you will flow rivers." How are you an outlet or channel through which he flows to the world? How do you encourage both inlets and outlets in the community you are leading?

4. "The Great Commission calls us not only to communist strongholds or hostile tribal chiefs but soccer moms and Starbucks baristas." Begin praying about the places around you and ask to see what God wants you to see. Make a list of where you see God already at work and join him there.

5. Reread and meditate on Romans 1:16, "For I am not ashamed of the gospel, because it is the power of God that brings salvation to everyone who believes." The gospel "is the power of God that brings salvation to everyone who believes." In what ways have you as a leader prioritized people knowing *about the gospel* over knowing *the person of God*?

5

EMPOWERED MOVEMENT

Foundation - Josh Harrison

∙ ∙

I've recently come to realize the body of Christ is larger than any one local church. This might seem obvious, not a stunning realization, but it's something I haven't given more than a passing thought for much of my life and career in ministry.

I've paid a lot of attention, especially as a pastor, to the importance of the local church—the fact that the Christian life cannot be lived in isolation, that we need one another to live and grow in this relationship with the Holy Spirit. All followers of Jesus must embed themselves deeply in and devote themselves passionately to a local church. This is not optional.

God calls us, Jesus saves us, and the Holy Spirit empowers us into community. If we are connected to the Vine, we are also connected to one another. If we find ourselves alone, disconnected from each other, there's a good chance we're not nearly as connected to the Vine as we thought we were. I've known and preached for a long time that being in community with one another is essential to living this empowered life. But what I haven't spent nearly enough time thinking, writing, or talking about (or practicing!) is the fact that *communities* in community with one another are essential as well.

In Ephesians 4, Paul wrote:

> Make every effort to keep the unity of the Spirit through the
> bond of peace. There is one body and one Spirit, just as you were
> called to one hope when you were called; one Lord, one faith, one
> baptism; one God and Father of all, who is over all and through
> all and in all. (Ephesians 4:3–6)

This is a powerful call not only to unity within a local church
community but across the global body of Christ. The cornerstone
of Paul's argument is a simple but profound truth: God is one.
Straight out of the book of Deuteronomy, this is the foundational
self-revelation of God to his people and, therefore, the primary way in
which he distinguishes his people from the rest of the world.

In the ancient world, people worshiped many gods. These gods
were inconsistent within themselves and incompatible with one
another. They were capricious in their emotions and actions. They
changed their minds, plans, desires, and expectations. They were
inscrutable and impossible to please. They reneged on their promises.
And because there were so many of them who were all equally
inconsistent, they were perpetually in conflict with one another, each
trying to thwart the other's plans for the world.

Imagine being a person living in the world of the gods. It was
impossible to know who they were and what they wanted, and
because they were so often fighting with one another, so were their
people. The history of the world is rife with people killing one another
in the names of their gods.

In this context, the truth that "God is one" is revolutionary
and revitalizing. He is completely integrous, wholly consistent in
character and mission. He is always true to himself and his plans for
and work in the world. And he alone is God. There is no other, no
rival to his throne, and, therefore, no one who can prevent him from
accomplishing everything he wants to do in the world.

With this truth firmly established, Paul continues: this God has a people, a family, who, in the words of his Son, are meant to be "one as we are [God is] one."

Because he is consistent, so are they. They all come to him in the same way (through faith). They all show the world they've entered into his family in the same way (through baptism, which is identification with the life, death, and resurrection of his Son). And they all receive power to live as his children and partner with him in the family business in the same way (through the enduring presence and power of his Spirit).

Because God is not in conflict with himself but is perfectly compatible within himself, united in the love shared among Father, Son, and Spirit, so are they. Despite their many differences they are made compatible by God, united to him and one another by his Holy Spirit.

In other words, God has not sent the Spirit into the world simply to adopt us as his children or even to bring us together into localized adopted families. He intends nothing less than a global body of Christ, a new humanity composed of stunning diversity, with people from every tribe, nation, language, and tongue worshiping one God, working toward one purpose, and devoting themselves to one family all by the power of his Spirit. The Holy Spirit is not in the business of empowering churches. He is in the business of empowering *the Church*, one global body to live and move together as *one* for the sake of the world he so loves.

In John 17, Jesus prayed like this:

> My prayer is not for them (the disciples) alone. I pray also for those who will believe in me through their message, that all of them may be one, Father, just as you are in me and I am in you. May they also be in us so that the world may believe that you have sent me. I have given them the glory that you gave me, that they may be one as we are one—I in them and you in me—so

that they may be brought to complete unity. Then the world will know that you sent me and have loved them even as you have loved me. (John 17:20–23)

Jesus made it clear here that his plan for saving the world involves "complete unity" within the body of Christ. This means our empowered communities cannot be who Jesus has created us to be or do what he has called us to do without being intimately connected to his global church. Just as no one Christian can fulfill Jesus' purposes without community, so too no one church, no matter how big or well-resourced, has all the tools necessary to "change the world" or even change our cities or neighborhoods without connection to and partnership with other churches.

I've come to realize this is especially true when our churches lack diversity. In communities where most of our members share the same ethnic/cultural background, socio-economic status, stage of life, and/or political leanings, the kind of radical, world-saving unity Jesus talks about in John 17 is not possible. We simply don't have all the resources we need. The Holy Spirit taught this to me in powerful ways during the last year.

I pastor a small church that, like many, struggles with diversity. We do have people from different socio-economic backgrounds and stages of life, but most of us come from the same ethnic and cultural background. The majority of our church is white.

I had been convinced for many years that diversity of all kinds within the local church is important and had longed to see it in my church, but I had no idea how to get there. Then I met Sheridan. Sheridan is the pastor of a largely black church that gathers a few miles up the road from our church. We met through a church-unity movement that is taking place in our county and over the last year have become dear friends. Through our friendship, our churches have become friends as well.

One of the most powerful expressions of this friendship is our monthly shared gatherings. On the last Sunday of every month, our two communities come together as one to worship, pray, and share a meal. I'll never forget the first time we did this. I remember standing at the back of our gathering, watching our two churches worship as one, and being moved to tears by what I was seeing: the body of Christ.

I realized two things in that moment: that my local church, as beautiful as it is, is only one part of that body; and that for most of my life with Jesus, because I had generally worshiped in churches like mine, with people who looked and acted and thought like me, I had only ever experienced that one part. When our two communities came together as one family, I got a fuller picture of Jesus' church and of him.

Jesus is so much bigger than our local church, so much more diverse and creative, so much more powerful. If we want to experience the fullness of the body of Christ, we must be in community with other communities.

And as we discussed in the last chapter, this experience of the body of Christ is not just for us. If we want the world to see the fullest picture of who Jesus is, we need more than our local church has to offer. Any accurate revelation of Jesus to the world demands a full body of Christ, a church of communities, empowered by the same Spirit moving together as one for the sake of the gospel.

In other words, our effectiveness in carrying out the mission Jesus has given us, and for which the Holy Spirit empowers us, is limited by our engagement with his global body. If we only ever participate in our local churches, we limit not only ourselves but also the world's experience of Jesus to one small part of his body. Conversely, as we come to know, love, walk with, work with, and pray for one another across the church, the global body of Christ, the world will see Jesus clearly and be transformed by his radical love.

We are not all that different from the people in the ancient world to whom Paul wrote Ephesians 4. We too live in a world of many gods who are as inconsistent and as incompatible as ever. The proposition that God is one is as refreshing and revitalizing as ever. And God's plan for demonstrating that oneness is the same as ever: It's us! It's his people, loyal to the same Lord, sharing the same faith, united through the same baptism, empowered by the same Spirit, beloved of the same Father. Remember John 17: "That they may be brought to complete unity. *Then* the world will know."

This is clearly a supernatural proposition, something we cannot do apart from the miraculous work of the Holy Spirit. Jesus' prayer in John 17 comes at the end of a conversation in which he promised the gift of the Holy Spirit (in John 14). Unity is only possible through this shared gift; there is no way we will be able to achieve this lofty vision without him.

At the same time, like everything else in the empowered life, the Holy Spirit will not force us into unity. He will not force us out of our local church to partner with the church across town. He will not force us to pursue fraternity with other followers of Jesus for the sake of our cities and nation. He will not force us to care about and pray for our sisters and brothers on the other side of the world. Because we are not simply recipients of but also partners with the Holy Spirit in this empowered life, we must choose to participate in this empowered movement he has been sent into the world to inspire.

Remember how Ephesians 4 starts: "*Make every effort* to keep the unity of the Spirit." The Spirit does the work of unity; we cannot do it without him. We must keep the unity he brings; he will not do it without us.

How do we do this? What "effort" must we invest if we want to experience the fullness of his body and be most effective in the mission to which he has called us?

First, we as leaders must dedicate ourselves to friendships with leaders from other communities. Start with the church next door. A phone call or meeting over a cup of coffee is often how great things get started. There may already be a group of pastors in your city who gather to support and pray for one another. If there is, join it. If there's not, start it. I have the privilege of participating in several such gatherings each month, and they have been transformative for me as a leader and for my church.

To paint a realistic picture, these unity gatherings are never convenient. They always "get in the way" of the work I need to be doing for my local church. Every time I attend one of these meetings, I feel like I don't have time for it. But I've come to realize it is my job not only to care for a local community of Spirit-filled Jesus followers but also to ensure my local community is connected to the larger body of Christ. If I do not, my local community will miss out on experiencing everything the church is and everything it can do when we function together as one. The truth is I don't have time not to be a part of these unity gatherings.

Second, look for ways the friendships you share as leaders can extend to your churches. Find ways to gather your churches together, to worship together, to pray together, to serve together, to eat together. You might be surprised at how powerful a simple meal can be when it is shared across communities.

Again, it will not be convenient. You will need to cancel other plans, find different venues, coordinate logistics, communicate clearly with your people. There will always be a thousand reasons not to participate in this empowered movement, but the one reason we ought to do so is more compelling than all of these combined: Jesus told us to, and this is how he intends to save the world.

Finally, pray. Prayer is the lifeblood of the body of Christ. We can do nothing without it. We cannot achieve anything we've talked about in this chapter (or this book) without the power of the Holy Spirit, so let's ask him to empower us for the sake of unity.

If you feel like you're on your own but you're hungry for the kind of fellowship I've been describing, then ask the Holy Spirit for some friends. None of the church-unity movements I'm a part of is something I initiated. The Holy Spirit provided all of them when I started to ask. He loves unity in the church, and he delights in answering this kind of prayer.

If you already have relationships with other leaders or communities, commit to praying for and with one another. These times of united prayer will be your deepest experience of the body of Christ *and* will be the most impactful for you, your community, and the world. You will never forget these shared prayer times and will always point back to them as pivotal moments in your life and ministry. This empowered movement into which we are invited begins, persists, grows, and will one day be completed through prayer.

Bridge – Todd Proctor

In this time when the world has never seemed more broken, one unexpected gift has been watching pastors and churches draw together in shared dependence in ways I have never experienced. Unity (dependence on each other) and prayer (dependence on God) have become hallmarks of this challenging season in beautifully redemptive ways.

As we trace the roots of empowered movements of the past, we stumble upon those who have been there and built there before. Those of us pastoring today stand on the shoulders of courageous, faith-filled leaders who banded together to help shape and shepherd past moves of the Spirit.

What follows is the story of my friend Chris Wienand. A native South African, Chris was caught up and raised up in aftershocks of the Jesus Movement to help lead a church-planting movement that resulted in hundreds of new communities being birthed around the world.

Chris is the embodiment of whatever it means to be an apostolic pioneer. He has spiritual sons and daughters in just about every major global city, and he continues to recruit orphaned and isolated leaders into the collaborative adventure of advancing the kingdom to the uttermost parts of the earth.

I'm grateful to have been one of many caught up in his catalytic wake years ago, and I can't imagine a better guide for leaders journeying together for the sake of more.

Frontiers – Chris Wienand

Chris Wienand is the founding leader of Genesis Collective, a global cohort of church planters based in Orange County, California.

In December of 1976, I began a vital, transformative redemption journey with Jesus. Since it was the '70s, my seminal faith was strongly influenced by the Jesus Movement and the Charismatic Renewal, both of which had swept into and through my hometown. I simply assumed "being saved" meant you did things like preaching on the streets, praying for the sick, and baptizing people in the ocean.

In those first naïve years, I expected the presence and power of the Holy Spirit to be evident in miracles, signs, and wonders. I and the others with whom I was sharing this new journey were living daily stories of a supernatural God breaking into our world with salvations, healings, provisions, and opening doors to church-planting adventures.

I recognized fairly quickly that the baptism of the Holy Spirit was not just about me stepping into the world of the supernatural for personal benefit and experience. It was beautifully obvious there was a communal piece to this power that transcended the "personal peace and prosperity" being presented as the popular message.

The book of Acts tells us there were around 120 Jesus followers gathered when the Holy Spirit arrived.[37] This was not just a singular moment; it was a gloriously collaborative awakening.

Fast-forwarding my story, in 1983 my wife, Meryl, and I planted our first church in Durban, South Africa. Neither of us was seminary-trained, but somehow we felt the Lord's hand on us. And we knew from the start that we needed much more than our own plans, tactics, and strategies.

We wholeheartedly believed Jesus when he said, "I tell you the truth: it is to your advantage that I go away, for if I do not go away, the Helper will not come to you. But if I go, I will send him to you" (John 16:7).

Anything Jesus said was worth his leaving for us to have, was something we wanted and knew we needed. You see, we can have all the plans, goals, and strategic steps, but unless "he comes" we are no different from a secular entrepreneurial initiative driven by human power.

"Come, Holy Spirit."

This was our little church's holy plea. We knew what our assignment was, and to do it, we needed more than we could muster. We weren't educated enough, old enough, wise enough, economically able enough. If this was going to work, we had to start at the very place Jesus started the early church—gathered in a room, praying with a deep hunger and holy desperation.

We had to learn about intercession, waiting prayer, listening prayer, supplication, and petitions. Oh, what glorious days, nights, and weeks of prayer and fasting we had as we cried, *"Come, Holy Spirit."*

What was the assignment we knew we needed the Holy Spirit and each other to accomplish?

He said to them . . . "But you will receive power when the Holy Spirit has come upon you, and you will be my witnesses in Jerusalem and in all Judea and Samaria, and to the end of the earth." (Acts 1:7–8)

Jesus essentially said, "Look, guys and gals, I am going to send you earth-shaking power, but this will be way more than a personal, X-factor, supernatural enrichment. I want you to look around your city and see what I can do when you join hands and hearts, to partner around my Spirit and see your city impacted."

I think these young Jews must have been so stoked. *What?* They must have thought. *We can change this beautiful Jerusalem of ours in your power?*

This is our first space: our church in our city. I have loved the deep relational glue that has knit churches together in all the cities in which I have pastored. Humility says, "I need you." In fact, Scripture says no person of a Jesus community can say to another, "I have no need of you."[38]

In Durban all those years ago, we knew the assignment was well beyond our one church community of Jesus followers. We started inviting other pastors and planters to come to the house we used as our home office. What began with four of us (and delicious chocolate cake) grew to include pastors and leaders driving from all over the city to gather. Together we prayed, worshiped, opened Scripture, lamented, ate, and grew in our love for Jesus and our love for each other.

This gathering characterized by hunger for more of the Holy Spirit forged friendships and partnership among pastors across our city, and it led to bringing our congregations together in celebration. By the time I relocated to the US, upward of two thousand people were gathering in Durban City Hall to worship together. There was a shared sense of faith and excitement seeing Jesus impacting our city.

Back to Acts 1. Jesus continued, perhaps after a pregnant pause, "And in all Judea."

Can you imagine this conglomerate of fishermen, tax collectors, homemakers, singles, marrieds, rich and poor, looking at each other with even greater surprise? *You mean we could transform the region around our city also?*

Jesus paused again, and then added in almost a whisper, "And Samaria."

I can imagine an audible gasp as these diligent Jews recoiled at the idea of engaging with the folks on the other side of the railroad tracks. *Us? There? Never!*

This is the second space of mission and collaboration: surrounding area with same culture (Judea) and surrounding area with different culture (Samaria).

We see this illustrated in Acts 19:

> On hearing this, they were baptized in the name of the Lord Jesus. When Paul placed his hands on them, the Holy Spirit came on them, and they spoke in tongues and prophesied. There were about twelve men in all. Paul entered the synagogue and spoke boldly there for three months, arguing persuasively about the kingdom of God. But some of them became obstinate; they refused to believe and publicly maligned the Way. So Paul left them. He took the disciples with him and had discussions daily in the lecture hall of Tyrannus. This went on for two years, so that all the Jews and Greeks who lived in the province of Asia heard the word of the Lord. (Acts 19:5–10)

What a story! A planting team of twelve, partnering with the Holy Spirit, triggered a regional awakening throughout all of Asia (Minor) within two years. Isn't it beautiful that the baptism of the Spirit was not just for personal blessing? The awakening had begun. Paul gathered them into a teaching arena and matched this Spirit encounter with the Word. They became a Word *and* Spirit community, and then they rushed this transformative gospel and reality out into the region.

Their goal wasn't to get more people into a building on a weekend. (In fact, they seemed to gather every day.) It was to "mobilize the many," to get everyone out on assignment together.

Back to Acts 1:8 once more. Jesus delivered the knock-out blow while his audience was still reeling: "And to the ends of the earth."

Imagine for a moment this group of people who had never traveled more than a few miles from their place of birth. This was like Jesus saying, "You will evangelize Mars." Stunned, skeptical, both zealous and reluctant, disbelieving, overwhelmed.

Haven't we all found ourselves here? Only when we reach a place of realizing the assignment is impossible in our own strength and resources, do we cry out in humility for his Holy Spirit to come.

And what Jesus said he would do, he did:

> Now an angel of the Lord said to Philip, "Go south to the road—the desert road—that goes down from Jerusalem to Gaza." So he started out, and on his way he met an Ethiopian eunuch, an important official in charge of all the treasury of the Kandake (which means "queen of the Ethiopians"). This man had gone to Jerusalem to worship, and on his way home was sitting in his chariot reading the book of Isaiah the prophet. The Spirit told Philip, "Go to that chariot and stay near it." (Acts 8:26–29)

Here the third space explodes on our screen. A eunuch from Africa encountered Jesus on a dusty road in a nowhere spot to be baptized. And the gospel went to the third space—the ends of the earth.

Don't you just love this gospel?

A true biblical awakening is when a group of leaders and Jesus lovers taste and touch this gospel in their city. The excitement and gratitude become so great that they splash into the second spaces and then the third. This message cannot be contained.

Meryl and I spent twenty-five years in a movement that planted churches in over sixty nations around the world. Seeded from the economic vulnerability of South Africa, we saw miracles upon miracles as new nations opened to Jesus. Movements are not the efforts of human plans, strategies, and actions. The fundamental underpinnings of a movement are stories upon stories of miracles only the Spirit of God can do.

May I give you some gentle suggestions for your own journey?

Become friends. We are not building organizations based on business principles. We are a Jesus-loving bunch of ragamuffins who want to hear the voice of the Spirit and obey.

Be patient. The writer of the book of Hebrews urges us to be "imitators of those who through faith and patience inherit the promises."[39] As with marriage, it is going to take some time to find trust, love, and a desire to collaborate. To rush is to lose; to be patient is to build something to hand on to our children.

Be humble. If we are to truly make an impact on our cities, counties, countries, and the uttermost with this beautiful gospel, we have to make humility our highest virtue.

When I was leading a church in Brea, California, we worked very hard to build relational trust with and throughout the city. Sometime into this journey we hosted an evening of combined worship. Weeks after the event, we learned our dear Baptist friend had spent the evening next to a very passionate, charismatic Jesus lover "singing in tongues" at the top of their voice. We talked through it and found a place of shared joy. This is the kind of bridge building we worked for daily. In time, the city council in Brea was so happy with what they were seeing that they told us they would pass no legislation that affected churches or families in Brea without first consulting us.

Be led. Leadership is essential to mobilizing an empowered movement. Awakenings need Spirit-led, humble men and women who will empower the many but continue to lead with their Father-given authority.

Be hungry. We have all read about revivals, reformations, and visitations that have straddled the globe at different times throughout the ages. None has been the same in content, leadership, and practice. What *has* been common is the cry, *"Come, Holy Spirit."* Isn't that amazing? An empowered movement costs. It costs prayers, passion, and priority. It costs individualism and consumerism. It costs pride and the need to be right.

Be honoring. There is a moment of relational harmony in Galatians 2:

> On the contrary, they recognized that I had been entrusted with the task of preaching the gospel to the uncircumcised, just as Peter had been to the circumcised. For God, who was at work in Peter as an apostle to the circumcised, was also at work in me as an apostle to the Gentiles. James, Cephas and John, those esteemed as pillars, gave me and Barnabas the right hand of fellowship when they recognized the grace given to me. They agreed that we should go to the Gentiles, and they to the circumcised. All they asked was that we should continue to remember the poor, the very thing I had been eager to do all along. (Galatians 2:7–10)

I love the honor, respect, and gift recognition this text offers. Wherever the movement mobilizes Jesus lovers, we must honor the wonderful and unique gifts carried by each. All are essential for impact.

Be together. Living the Spirit-led life and mission is not a solo endeavor. History repeatedly reminds us that none of us can achieve this work alone. It is an "us" story, a "we" story. There were 120 early believers gathering daily in deep and hungry prayer. That is where this empowered movement started. We were meant to be empowered together.

Every reader of the book of Acts is left with a question: *God, will you do it again?* And perhaps a corollary: *Can we collectively be part of one more awakening in our time?*

From forty-two years of walking with the Spirit and being involved in five global Spirit awakenings, I know absolutely that God *can.* It's up to us whether he does.

There are no rules but listening and obeying. There is no formula but humility and unity. There are no experts but those who cry out together in hunger:

"Come, Holy Spirit."

REFLECTION QUESTIONS

1. When was the last time you gathered with another group of church leaders or another church to encourage each other and pray together? Ask God to lead you to be part of an empowered movement in your community. Is there already a group of pastors or ministry leaders who meet nearby to encourage each other and pray for one another? If so, join it. If not, start one.

2. How is your church limited in its experience of the body of Christ by its diversity (or lack thereof)? What conversation can you have with someone of a different background this week for the sake of unity across the global church body?

3. How do we keep the unity of the Spirit as Paul instructs in Ephesians 4? What are some ways we can practice this not only in our own churches but across our city and around the world?

4. The Holy Spirit is not just for personal blessing but to mobilize the many, to be empowered together. What would it require of you to be part of another awakening in your time? To say, *"Come, Holy Spirit."*

6

EMPOWERED MOMENT

Foundation - Josh Harrison

. . . .

The power of this empowered life is relationship. This is the bedrock principle of this book. In our foundational passage, John 14, Jesus described the Holy Spirit not simply as "the Advocate," but "*another* Advocate." He intended for his disciples to understand that their experience of life with the Holy Spirit would be similar to their experience of life with him.

What did their life with Jesus look like? Relationship. They walked with him, talked with him, ate with him, learned from him, and argued with him. They were amazed by him, confused by him, inspired by him, infuriated by him. They had great days with him and terrible days with him and a lot of days that were somewhere in between. In other words, they lived in relationship with Jesus.

We could describe our close relationships with people in much the same way. This is why I so appreciate Eugene Peterson's translation of John 14:16: "I will talk to the Father, and he'll provide you another *Friend* so that you will always have someone with you."[40] While I prefer the NIV translation for the reasons discussed in the preface, I think Peterson beautifully captures the kind of "Advocate" we have. It is our friend who calls out from alongside us, reminding us of and empowering us to be who we are.

This relational framework, this friendship with the Holy Spirit, is essential to our understanding and experience of life with him. So often I think we approach the Holy Spirit as a special phenomenon reserved for weekend services and special prayer meetings. Our lives with him consist of chasing him from mountaintop to mountaintop, from powerful moment to powerful moment. The problem is that when we do this, we miss out on his best work.

A mountaintop is a wonderful thing—fresh air, inspiring views, and you can see for miles in every direction. But nothing grows on a mountaintop. Planting, growing, tending, and harvesting all happen in valleys. In other words, life happens in the valleys. And that's what we're really interested in here: *life* with the Holy Spirit, not just moments.

Our hope in this book has been to normalize and routinize our lives with him. This is not to say he is ordinary or bland. Far from it! He is still Holy God, and we must never lose sight of that. May we never become so familiar with him that we think of him as less than everything he is. In fact, holding both of these truths in dynamic tension—that he is both Holy God and our friend—ought to inspire us to new heights of awe and worship *and* new expectancy in our daily lives.

When we speak of "normal" or "routine" life with him, we are not demeaning him but are elevating our normal and routine. We are seeking to live our everyday lives with an ever-growing awareness of his presence, anticipation of his power, and experience of his love for us and for the world into which he has sent us. We are interested in what Mike Pilavachi and Andy Croft call the "everyday supernatural."[41] If we are in relationship with God, every day is filled with the supernatural and every moment with potential.

That said, not all moments are equal. This is true in all our significant relationships. Most days are fairly normal: spending ordinary time together, growing in love through simple shared presence. But in every meaningful relationship, these ordinary days and years are punctuated by extraordinary moments. These moments serve both to define the relationship and propel it forward into new intimacy and joy. This is why it is essential in any relationship not only to commit ourselves to daily faithfulness in the normal and routine, but also to cultivate and pursue meaningful moments actively.

This is also true of our relationship with the Holy Spirit. Much of this life with him will take place in the normal and every day. But there will be moments along the way when his presence is especially palpable, his power especially evident. Every so often, he will lead us out of the valley to a mountaintop where we breathe the fresh air, get inspired by the glory all around, and see clearly where we've been and where we're going. These mountaintop moments often mark a change of season and move us forward into new places both in our relationship with God and our understanding of ourselves.

This is true not only on a personal level but also on a community level. Remember, this empowered life is not a solo venture. It is a shared journey. We are part of a body, all filled and empowered by the same Spirit, growing in relationship with him together, walking through valleys together, sometimes even ascending mountaintops together. And when we are truly committed to the community of the Spirit, not only to our local expression but also to the global body of Christ and its mission in the world, these shared mountaintop experiences take a special form and name: "revival."

Depending on your church context and history, this word may be loaded with all sorts of connotations, both positive and negative. But I use the word here simply to refer to a unique outpouring of the Holy Spirit that begins in a specific, often localized context, but it quickly extends beyond that place to inspire a global movement and empower a new era in the church.

History is rife with such revivals. The first of these, of course, was the day of Pentecost itself. But contrary to what some may claim, it was not the last. Throughout the centuries, the Holy Spirit has continued to show up in these unique *empowered moments* to reinvigorate, redefine, and—importantly—expand his church.

In 1722, Count Nicholas von Zinzendorf graciously allowed a small band of religious fugitives, Christians from Moravia (in modern-day Czech Republic), to settle on his land. Zinzendorf was an amazing man with a deep, burning passion for Jesus that burned even hotter when he was surrounded by these Moravian exiles. He would go on to rename his estate (in present day Germany) Herrnhut, which means, "the Lord's Watch." It became a thriving village and church.

On August 13, 1727, Zinzendorf was leading a baptism and communion service. As he was praying passionately in front of the congregation, the Holy Spirit fell on the community, binding the whole church together with an overwhelming sense of love and mission. Out of this service, the church decided to begin a 24/7 prayer chain that would run unbroken for over one hundred years. Every hour of every day, there was a member of this Moravian church praying for their community. Their specific collective prayer was that God would raise up workers from within their community to take the gospel to the ends of the earth. And he did!

Within a year, they sent their first two missionaries to the West Indies islands of St. Thomas and St. Croix. Today we know these places as amazing vacation destinations, but at the time they were slave colonies, a stopover for African slaves on their way to the Americas. As the prayer chain rolled on, so did the Moravian mission. Over the course of one generation, this empowered little church sent out more than three hundred missionaries to unreached people around the world in the West Indies, Greenland, Lapland, Turkey, and North America.[42]

The Moravians had a tremendous influence on several key figures in Christian history, including a man named William Carey who became known as the "father of modern missions." Carey spent his life as a missionary in India. While there, he wrote a small book called *An Inquiry into the Obligation of Christians to Use Means for the Conversion of the Heathen*. A strange, not terribly politically correct title, I know, but it was this book that five students at Williams

College in Massachusetts met to discuss on a blustery afternoon in August of 1806.

They met in the middle of a meadow north of their campus to read Carey's book, discuss it together, and pray. While they were meeting, a thunderstorm broke overhead, and they were forced to run for cover. They found shelter underneath a haystack in the middle of the field. Rather than give up their meeting, though, they kept right on going through the storm.

Their conversation centered around what it would look like to reach the unreached people of China. The leader of the group, a man named Samuel Mills, was particularly passionate and pleaded and prayed at great length for the lost in China. At one point, yelling over thunderclaps, Mills prayed, "O God, strike down the arm, with the red artillery of heaven, that shall be raised against a herald of the cross." When they had finished praying, Mills looked up, reportedly with flashes of lightning reflecting in his eyes, and cried out, "We can do this, if we will!" At that moment, the Spirit of God fell and something broke loose in the hearts of all five. Later, all pointed back to that prayer meeting, which came to be known as the Haystack Prayer Meeting, as the defining moment in their lives. All five dedicated themselves wholeheartedly to world missions, and out of that one meeting came the greatest global missions movement the world had ever seen.

From this small gathering of five men, several world-changing missions agencies were launched: the United Foreign Missionary Society, the American Baptist Missionary Union, and the United Bible Societies. Within a generation, more than twenty thousand missionaries had been mobilized and sent from the United States around the world.

Prior to the Haystack Prayer Meeting, global missions from the US were virtually non-existent. Within eighty years, a man named Luther Wishard would begin an organization called the Student Volunteer Movement that would result in the mobilization of over

100,000 college students across the world in global missions. Today, the fruits of the Haystack Prayer Meeting are incalculable.[43]

In the 1850s, the US was in a bad place spiritually, morally, and economically (sound familiar?). Particularly in New York City, crime and moral depravity were on the rise and unemployment rates were skyrocketing. More than thirty thousand men were unemployed. This doesn't sound like a lot to us today, but in a city with a population, at the time, around one million, that's a lot of people without jobs.

In 1857, a man named Jeremiah Lanphier took a position within the Dutch Reformed denomination as a "city missionary" to the city of New York. Knowing the enormity of the challenges facing him in his role and burdened by the needs around him, Lanphier did the only thing he knew how to do: he started praying. In fact, he decided to start a prayer meeting. He created handouts and distributed them around the city. Here's what they said:

HOW OFTEN SHALL I PRAY?

As often as the language of prayer is in my heart; as often as I see my need of help; as often as I feel the power of temptation; as often as I am made sensible of any spiritual declension or feel the aggression of a worldly spirit.

In prayer we leave the business of time for that of eternity, and intercourse with men for intercourse with God.

A day Prayer Meeting is held every Wednesday, from 12 to 1 o'clock, in the Consistory building in the rear of the North Dutch Church, corner of Fulton and William Streets (entrance from Fulton and Ann Streets).

This meeting is intended to give merchants, mechanics, clerks, strangers, and business men generally an opportunity to stop and call upon God amid the perplexities incident to their respective avocations. It will continue for one hour; but it is also designed for those who may find it inconvenient to remain more than five or ten minutes, as well as for those who can spare the whole hour.

The first meeting was held on September 23, 1857. Lanphier opened the door precisely at noon and discovered, to his dismay, that no one had come. So he prayed and paced. Five minutes passed. No one showed. Ten minutes, fifteen minutes, twenty, twenty-five. Finally, at twelve-thirty, Lanphier heard someone coming up the stairs, and the first person appeared. Over the next few minutes, four more showed up. They held their first prayer meeting with six people.

Despite the group's small size, the Holy Spirit was there, and the meeting was powerful. Lanphier decided to hold the meeting again the next week and was shocked when he arrived to find forty people waiting and ready to pray. That day, they decided to begin meeting daily rather than weekly.

Within six months, ten thousand businessmen were gathering each day to pray in downtown New York City. Keep in mind, ten thousand a day out of a population of one million. Within two years, over one million people were added to churches across the US, churches that just two years earlier had been on the verge of closing their doors. One million people![44]

In 1904 a dramatic movement of the Holy Spirit occurred in Wales. At the turn of the century, Wales was in much the same spot the US had been in in the 1850s: church decline, economic difficulties, rising crime rates, and alcoholism. In the spring of 1904, after hearing a traveling evangelist speak in his town, a young man named Evan Roberts found himself routinely waking up early in the morning. Being awake and unable to go back to sleep, he would simply start praying. He prayed for revival among his people every morning from 1:00 a.m. until 5:00 a.m.

I won't tell the whole story, but the short version is this: the Spirit of God descended on Wales. In a few short years, more than 150,000 people came to Jesus. Churches were bursting at the seams and crime rates decreased to almost nothing. Strangely, bankruptcies among local businesses increased as almost every bar in the area went out of business.

The Welsh Revival, as it came to be known, did not end in Wales. It swept across the country and jumped oceans, spawning other revivals in Britain, Scandinavia, Europe, North America, India, East Asia, Africa, and Latin America.

In 1906, an African American preacher named William Seymour traveled from Houston to Los Angeles for a one-month preaching residency at an area church. On February 25, Seymour preached his first sermon in Los Angeles: the topic was on speaking in tongues and the work of the Holy Spirit. He returned to the church the next Sunday to find a padlock had been placed on the door. He was no longer welcomed—or supported—because the church had deemed his teaching on the Holy Spirit to be dangerous and heretical (based on the fact that none of them had ever experienced what Seymour was talking about).

However, not all the members of the church rejected Seymour. He was invited to stay in the home of one of the church members. And while he tried to save up some money to return home to Houston, he began leading a Bible study and prayer meeting in this home. During one of those meetings, following a ten-day fast, the Holy Spirit filled those gathered in the house in a completely new way. Just like in the book of Acts, the meeting spilled out into the street, and Seymour started preaching from the balcony of the house to crowds of people who gathered to see what was going on.

Very quickly the gathering outgrew the house and was forced to move into the Azusa Street Mission. There they began holding around-the-clock worship services, which continued for nearly seven years and took the city and the world by storm. Azusa Street gave birth to the Pentecostal movement which now, just over one hundred years later, accounts for nearly 25 percent of the world's Christians.

In Pyongyang (in what is now North Korea) in 1907, a group of twenty missionaries began meeting together weekly to pray for their work in Korea. Everything was stacked against them. Pyongyang was a sort of center of moral depravity. The Koreans were living under the brutal military rule of the Japanese and, as a result, carried tremendous bitterness toward the Japanese. The missionaries had been working hard but seeing very little fruit. So they started praying.

They prayed for weeks before they began to see breakthroughs. Their prayer gatherings started to grow in numbers and frequency; they started meeting daily, crying out to God together, confessing their sins to one another, and pleading to God on behalf of their country. During one prayer service, one of the missionaries started praying and got no further than, "Father! Father!" when according to him, "It seemed as if the roof was lifted from the building and the Spirit of God came down from heaven in a mighty avalanche of power upon us."

Within three years, more than 250,000 Christians were meeting in thousands of churches across Korea, despite violent oppression from the occupying Japanese. When the communist regime took over North Korea, Christians were forced to flee south, but they took the revival with them. In 1954, a young Buddhist dying of tuberculosis was powerfully healed and led to Christ. His name was Yonggi Cho, and he would go on to plant a church that is, today, the largest Pentecostal church in the world with nearly a half-million members: Yoido Full Gospel Central Church. Today, South Korea is one of the largest missionary-sending countries in the world.[45]

And these are just a few of many examples. I've said nothing of the Chinese House Church Movement, the Jesus Movement, the Toronto Blessing, or Iran's Great Awakening, to name a few.

I believe more of these empowered moments are coming. In fact, the US is seemingly poised for a new revival, a fresh outpouring of the Holy Spirit. The last few years have been tumultuous ones for the American church. Political polarization, shifting cultural values, social unrest, a global pandemic, and so many other factors have all resulted in unprecedented fissures within the body of Christ. And because unity is such an important part of our evangelistic effectiveness, we are seeing a record decline in the American church. In fact, for the first time in our history as a nation, church membership has fallen below 50 percent. What this tells us is that the American church has become entrenched and institutionalized, and it is in desperate need of a new awakening if we hope to reach the world with the gospel of the kingdom. The time is ripe for another empowered moment.

But the Holy Spirit will not simply do it to us. Remember, he does not empower unwilling people. Just as we must participate in our daily lives with the Holy Spirit, so too must we participate with him in these empowered moments. If we want to be part of one of these unique moves of the Spirit of God that breaks up the hard soil of an entrenched church and enables it to touch people who were previously beyond its reach, we must cultivate the moment.

How do we do this? Through prayer. Take everything we've talked about in these pages—a deep and growing understanding of his love, a repentant heart, a disciplined faith, participation in his church, availability for mission, commitment to unity with his body—and add to it persistent, prevailing prayer, and we will see a new revival.

The first outpouring of the Holy Spirit on the day of Pentecost began with a group of disciples gathered in prayer, and, as far as I'm aware, every move of God since has followed suit. Every revival throughout history has looked different and has been uniquely contextualized to the time, location, and circumstances in which it has taken place. But one thing is constant: every one, without fail, has begun and persisted in prayer. For the Moravians, the 24/7 prayer chain transformed their community and the world. Five men praying under a haystack during a thunderstorm gave birth to the modern missions movement. In New York City, a group of six people gathering in prayer was the spark that ignited a national revival. In Wales, when asked the secret behind the revival, Evan Roberts replied, without hesitation, "My brother, there is no secret! Ask and you shall receive!" Azusa Street began and continued as a worship and prayer meeting. And nothing that happened in Korea would have happened apart from those twenty missionaries gathered in prayer.

Right before Jesus promised his disciples the power of the Holy Spirit and commissioned them to be his witness "in Jerusalem, Judea and Samaria, and to the ends of the earth" (Acts 1:8), he told them to go back to Jerusalem and wait for the gift he had promised: the gift of the Holy Spirit. They understood "wait" to mean "pray." And as a result of their waiting and praying, the Spirit came, and the world was forever changed.

We are here today as a result of those prayers. Now it's our turn. This is our moment. Let's pray.

Bridge – Todd Proctor

For me, these accounts of leaders who modeled an impassioned, unyielding commitment to prayer are equally inspiring and intimidating. It is powerful to be reminded throughout history of ways faith-filled sparks of a few became raging bonfires that spiritually reshaped nations. Yet I find myself wondering, What does this really look like today? Or perhaps the better question, Who does this look like? It seems so many pastors on the rise are far more celebrated for their snowballing social media empires than the slow, secret work of sustained intercession.

This is why I remember so well my first meeting with Jon Tyson. I was a young leader of a Southern California megachurch on the hunt for the latest best practice in multi-site strategy. This quest took me across the country to the Manhattan office of an even younger pastor with a unique, parish-based vision for multiplication.

A few minutes into our conversation, it became clear he was dreaming much bigger dreams than launching a few more church gatherings. His heart was captured by and broken for his city. He longed to be part of a movement of God that strategy might shape but only the Spirit could empower. So he was committed to walking and praying the streets of Hell's Kitchen each morning, sowing daily seeds of faith and desperation for the sake of the harvest yet to come.

More than any words he spoke (which were undeniably eloquent with his cool Aussie accent), I left our conversation most impacted by his example of simple perseverance. His willingness to keep showing up in prayer seemed to pave the way for God's willingness to keep showing up in power.

Over the years, our growing friendship and shared adventures have given me the proximity to watch God amplify Jon's voice and vision not only across the Big Apple but throughout the world. The steady rise of his ministry influence has been matched by a deepening commitment to invest in intercession—to lead from his knees. Here, he describes some practical and powerful ways prayer has been the key to "calling out the future" of his city.

Frontiers - Jon Tyson

Jon Tyson is the planter and lead pastor of Church of the City in New York City.

In some ways, it feels like forever ago that my family and I moved to New York. In other ways, it feels like yesterday. It's been a remarkable journey.

Along the way, a few folks have asked me if I would be willing to share some of the most valuable lessons I have learned while planting here in New York. As you read these reflections, please know I'm not trying to make things sound better than they are or say we have all the answers. This is my humble and honest attempt to give words to what we have learned and seen God do in our midst.

Of all the lessons I've learned, the most important, hands down, is the primal priority of seeking God through prayer. Karl Barth once said, "To clasp the hands in prayer is the beginning of an uprising against the disorder of this world."

The most important part of that quote is the word "beginning." Most church planters want to begin with strategy, mission, outreach, contextualization studies, theology, or small groups. As necessary as these things are, the first should always be prayer. Paul writes in Colossians 4:

> Devote yourselves to prayer, being watchful and thankful. And pray for us, too, that God may open a door for our message, so that we may proclaim the mystery of Christ, for which I am in chains. (Colossians 4:2–3)

I have tried to take this verse literally every day for the last seven years, but I was particularly keen in the beginning to make sure that not only was our church built on prayer but that prayer became an inseparable part of the culture of the church.

Here are some of the things we did, have done, and continue to do to make this a reality.

We were living in Orlando when we began sensing God might be calling us to start a church in New York. The first thing we did was a forty-day fast. We wanted to get real clarity that this wasn't just a good idea, a unique opportunity, or our own ambition. We wanted to know this was something God was asking us to do. Sensing it would be hard, we wanted to know that regardless of the outcome, our very presence and lives would be acts of worship and obedience. On the last day of the fast, I got a check for ten thousand dollars in the mail. An anonymous person felt led to give it to us so we could pay off any debt and move forward in the direction God was leading us.

Once we felt we had clarity, we gathered a small group of people together for nights of prayer, worship, and discussion. Those early days of seeking God, offering up sincere, hopeful prayers of faith, and believing the promises of God together were vital in setting the culture. We did this before we ever talked about programs, strategy, mission, or anything else.

When we first moved to the city, we planned to go without office space. We did this for two reasons: cost savings and the chance to meet people. When we did get an office, it wasn't so we could "run our church;" it was so we could establish a base for intercessory prayer. We rented one small room just off Times Square. Although we didn't know it at the time, it was between two sex establishments. It was as shady as you can imagine, but it was also a place to pray.

When I was the only full-time staff member, I would go to the office and spend whole days praying, fasting, worshiping, and asking God to move in the city. The presence of God was often so tangible it seemed impossible. That place felt like a portal between heaven and earth, so we decided to invite others in.

We began to host half-nights of prayer every Friday on the roof of our offices. The roof was incredible, with a panoramic view over midtown Manhattan. We would worship, cry out to God, savor his goodness, and claim his promises over the city. We saw some miraculous answers to those prayers, and it cultivated a deep sense of awe and faith that we were not on our own or making the whole thing up.

One year, we felt prompted during the season of Lent to gather our pastors and spend three hours a day praying for spiritual breakthrough in our ministry. We broke the Lord's prayer into six thirty-minute segments and met at our East Village offices. This was completely impractical, tiring, and amazing. One morning we prayed for one of our friends to come to Christ; he did that afternoon. One of our pastors needed fifty thousand dollars within a week; he got it six days later. It was one of those shared, beautiful times when the promises of God leaped off the pages of the Bible and wrote themselves into the scripts of our lives.

When we got ready to plant our Brooklyn church, the leadership community of our three churches in Manhattan gathered, worshiped, took communion, and then walked the neighborhood in small teams asking God for spiritual doors to open, for blessing on the community, and that his kingdom would come in Park Slope as it is in heaven.

Before we planted our East Village church, we sent out more than eighty people who prayed over every street in the neighborhood as a base of spiritual life for all that would happen in the years to come.

In Washington Heights, we have hosted a prayer meeting for the last four years on Monday nights. These gatherings are a time to seek God for transformation in this vital neighborhood, where there was a commitment to three years of prayer before we launched our neighborhood church there.

Our Tribeca church prayed faithfully in the neighborhood for a year and a half before launching a gathering, and the first thing the community did was meet for prayer.

I have regularly taken two hours a day to pray through various neighborhoods of the city, and to worship and declare the goodness and glory of God over the city. This prayer is more intercessory and is contesting for the lordship of Jesus. This practice is also a key tool for discipling leaders; I invite them to join me, and I get to impart a heart and vision for praying, seeking God, and claiming promises in their lives.

We have regularly participated in a weekly pastors' prayer meeting for leaders across the city to build unity, break down selfish ambition, and seek God for spiritual awakening here in New York.

We have helped gather churches from across the city for nights dedicated to worship and prayer for our city, and to create a wider culture of prayer and seeking God throughout the church in New York.[46]

I have regularly devoted Tuesday afternoons to secret seasons of prayer. I ask God for more humility, spiritual power, insight into the Scriptures, a heart for him, and the salvation of my unbelieving friends and neighbors. Having a chunk of time to pray over my sermon, over the city, and for salvation for others has been a source of deep joy and sustainability for me.

For several weeks God spoke to me through the Scriptures around the idea of keys—small pieces of metal with the power to open massive doors. Keys give access to what's behind doors. Keys symbolize authority and so much more.

I shared in one pastors' meeting that I felt God was giving us some keys to ministry through the idea of viewing prayer as a key. Then one Sunday after I finished preaching, a member of our congregation pulled me aside and said something to the effect of, "I know this may sound weird, but I feel like God wants you to know he is giving you prayer as a key to his work in the city. On a recent trip overseas I got this key and I'm pretty sure I'm supposed to give it to you as a tangible sign of what God wants to do through prayer." The key I was handed was a beautiful antique key. I was blown away by God's tangible confirmation that the "eyes of the LORD are on the righteous, and his ears are attentive to their prayers."[47]

I could share literally hundreds of amazing answers to prayer from the past seven years. From salvation for lost friends to the healing of a staff member, financial provision, and on and on, the joy of partnering with God through prayer has been the foundation of all that we do.

From the opening page of Scripture to its last, God's heart has been to hear the cries of his people and respond on their behalf. At this strategic time in history, in this city we call home, we have passionately tried to take God up on his invitation. I hope in some tangible way, these few paragraphs inspire you to do the same.

I close with the ever-inspiring quote on intercessory prayer from Walter Wink:

> Intercession visualizes an alternative future to the one apparently fated by the momentum of current forces. Prayer infuses the air of a time yet to be into the suffocating atmosphere of the present. History belongs to the intercessors who believe the future into being. . . . Even a small number of people, firmly committed to

the new inevitability on which they have fixed their imaginations, can decisively affect the shape the future takes. These shapers of the future are the intercessors, who call out of the future the longed-for new present.[48]

REFLECTION QUESTIONS

1. Josh talks about normalizing the Holy Spirit in our lives by elevating our normal. What would elevating your normal be for you personally? For your family? For your church team?

2. Mountaintop moments often mark a change of season and move us forward in our relationship with God. What experiences have you had recently that you would identify as mountaintop moments?

3. Intentional, passionate prayer was the fundamental force behind the great empowered movements of the Holy Spirit. How will you use this moment in our culture to cultivate another empowered movement in your community?

4. Depending on your church role, what changes in the predictable routine of your church can you make to make your church more resemble the ignited church of Acts?

CONCLUSION

Todd Proctor

. . . .

Among those reading these stories of empowered life and leadership, I imagine reactions are all over the map. Excitement. Skepticism. Curiosity. And perhaps confirmation, good or bad, of your own past experiences.

For some, this is familiar territory. For others, this is foreign ground waiting to be cautiously explored. As reflected in these chapters, this is not only a pastoral journey but a personal one as well, rarely marked by straight paths or level ground. The invitation to embrace more dependence on and empowerment of the Spirit is a call to off-road adventures. We can assume unexpected twists, turns, and forks in the road that inevitably lead us far beyond our own comfort and capacity.

But the collective hope of these authors is that one conviction becomes crystal clear: there is more.

A cry first captured in song by British church planter and renowned worship leader Tim Hughes decades ago is now ours to claim:

> There must be more than this, oh breath of God, come breathe within.
> There must be more than this, Spirit of God, we wait for you.
> Fill us anew we pray. Fill us anew we pray.[49]

"Fill us anew." Yes! As we navigate the complex, compounding challenges of this time, we need to be filled with whatever confidence, clarity, and authority God has to give. Our best is simply not enough. And for far too long, the Western church has drifted deeper and deeper into an identity crisis—forgetting and forsaking our intended design and directive.

We act as if we're on a cruise ship. I'm old enough to remember a '70s TV series called *The Love Boat.* Each week we were invited onboard the *Pacific Princess* to watch a new group of passengers gathered, welcomed, and entertained by an attentive, winsome, casually-cool crew with feathered hair and short shorts.

Plot points varied slightly with each episode, but the backdrop rarely changed. Same boat. Same amenities. Same meals. Same stops. Same bright smile from the charismatic, celebrity captain who was impeccably uniformed but rarely called to do more than stroll the decks, shake hands, and offer inspiring toasts on cue.

The goal of the *Pacific Princess*—or any cruise ship for that matter—seemed to be to project the illusion of high seas adventure while ensuring a reality of safety, comfort, and constant customer satisfaction.

In sad but true fashion, it's easy to recognize some of these same plot markers in the evolution of what millions have come to know as "doing church." Gatherings are filled with unstated expectations of comfort, convenience, entertainment, and inspiration—all designed to approximate a sense of life-changing adventure. But in reality, this becomes an all-too predictable route that drops us off right where—and as—we began.

The church incubated and ignited in the book of Acts bears little resemblance to this picture. If we stick with the water vessel metaphor, it seems like a *Pirates of the Caribbean*-type galleon would be a far better comparison. Those ships were not designed for consumeristic comfortability. They were built for navigating high seas with the assumption of weathering storms. Passengers were usually expected to become crew and serve in specific roles for the good of the whole. And the voyage itself was not one of circuitous sightseeing but one of risk-taking adventure. Destinations were often unknown, but new frontiers awaited discovery and stewardship.

Such a vessel is dead in the water without the wind. A sailboat of any size is utterly dependent on the gust that fills its sails to propel it forward. And amidst many unique assignments, the collective responsibility of the crew is to be prepared and positioned to catch the wind well. They can't create the wind. They can't control the wind. But the ability to *catch* the wind is essential to getting to wherever "there" is.

We live and lead in a moment when catching the wind of the Spirit has never seemed more important to the church moving forward. The stories you've read here bear witness to what it can look like to discover through dependence that adventure awaits! You may feel tossed by the waves or even stuck in a dead calm. But for those who charted the course of the church in her earliest moments, their best (and only) option was to wait for "the Wind."

The instructions of Jesus were clear:

> What comes next is very important: I am sending what my Father promised to you, so stay here in the city until he arrives, until you're equipped with power from on high. (Luke 24:49 MSG)

In this time of division and disorientation, what comes next is very important—too important to navigate without the empowerment of the one who was promised and sent. From the outset, the church was designed and destined to fail unless he showed up.

So let's catch the wind together for the sake of the future, and let's give voice for a new generation to the prayer that has echoed across two millennia:

"Come, Holy Spirit. Empower us to more."

NOTES

1. *My Utmost for His Highest* by Oswald Chambers (Barbour Books: 1963).

2. "Reflections," in *Christianity Today* (Dec. 13, 1985).

3. *The Knowledge of the Holy* by A. W. Tozer (General Press: 2019).

4. To be clear, I am pro-adoption regardless of the path it takes to get there. Whether it is your Plan A, your Plan B, or your Plan Z, if God is putting adoption in front of you, go after it!

5. In both Hebrew and Greek, the word we translate as "Spirit" literally means "wind."

6. NIV translation.

7. Romans 8:16.

8. 2 Corinthians 5:17.

9. John 14:16.

10. Colossians 3:12; Galatians 3:13–14; Galatians 4:7; Titus 3:7; Romans 8:38–39.

11. I'm not sure if Terry's ever written these words or even if they were originally his. I heard him say this during a prayer gathering at Rock Harbor Church in Costa Mesa, California, in 2014.

12. As quoted in *If God Be for Us: Sermons on the Gifts of the Gospel* (Harper: 1954) by Robert Edward Luccock. This may be a variant translation or paraphrase of an excerpt from his 169th sermon: "He who created you without you will not justify you without you."

13. "Jesus, Take the Wheel" is a song written by Brett James, Hillary Lindsey, and Gordie Sampson, and recorded by Carrie Underwood (Artista: 2005).

14. *Mere Christianity* by C. S. Lewis (HarperOne: 2015).

15. Galatians 5:16.

16. Romans 8:15.

17. *Prince Caspian* by C. S. Lewis (HarperCollins: 2002).

18. "Live Life to the Full" by Dallas Willard (https://dwillard.org/articles/live-life-to-the-full).

19. Hebrews 4:15.

20. *Matthew: A Commentary, Volume 1: The Christbook, Matthew 1–12* by Fredrick Dale Bruner (Zondervan: 2014), as quoted in *The Ruthless Elimination of Hurry* by John Mark Comer (WaterBrook: 2019).

21. *Pleasures Evermore: The Life-Changing Power of Enjoying God* by Sam Storms (NavPress: 2000).

22. He went on to discuss the fact that many of the commandments remain unfulfillable because of the absence of a Jewish temple on Mount Zion, a particularly controversial and politically/religiously charged assertion with significant real-world consequences.

23. *A Greek-English Lexicon* compiled by Henry George Liddell and Robert Scott (Oxford University Press: 1996).

24. *Exegetical Dictionary of the New Testament* edited by Horst Balz and Gerhard Schneider (T&T Clark: 1990).

25. *Lexicon of the New Testament* by Johannes Louw and Eugene Nida (United Bible Society: 1988).

26. 1 Corinthians 12.

27. Megan Marshman discusses this story briefly in her book *Meant for Good* (Zondervan: 2020), but I'm recounting further details from a conversation I had with her.

28. I use the term "sons" not to be chauvinistic but because this is what Paul does in Romans 8. When Paul says the Holy Spirit has

"brought about [our] adoption to *sonship*," he does not intend to exclude women but rather to include them in the sons' inheritance. In a context where only male children inherited family fortune and business, Paul says that all who are filled with the Spirit, both women and men, are sons—full heirs of all rights, privileges, and responsibilities that come with the family name.

29. Quoted from *Josephus,* translated by H. St. J. Thackeray (Harvard University Press: 1961).

30. Ephesians 6:12.

31. *The Spirit of Christ* by Andrew Murray (Whitaker House: 2010).

32. If we assume a relational understanding of this empowered life, there is no conflict between John 20 and Acts 1–2. They had received the Holy Spirit when Jesus breathed on them, yet they had to wait for his coming on the day of Pentecost. And as the book of Acts and the history of the church clearly show, Pentecost would not be their last encounter with the Holy Spirit.

33. Acts 2:11.

34. Adapted from Craig Springer's *How to Revive Evangelism: 7 Vital Shifts in How We Share Our Faith* (Grand Rapids: Zondervan, 2020).

35. *Reviving Evangelism*, 56.

36. These ideas came out of a conversation I had with my friend Jay Pathak, pastor of Mile High Vineyard. Check out his book *The Art of Neighboring.*

37. Acts 1:14–15; 2:1–4.

38. 1 Corinthians 12:21.

39. Hebrews 6:12, ESV.

40. The Message translation.

41. Pilavachi and Croft have written an amazing book on life with the Holy Spirit with this title (David C. Cook: 2016).

42. If you'd like to learn more about Zinzendorf and Moravian movement, start with this short article from *Christianity*

Today: https://www.christianitytoday.com/history/people/denominationalfounders/nikolaus-von-zinzendorf.html. Or visit the Moravian Church's website: https://www.moravian.org/2018/07/a-brief-history-of-the-moravian-church/.

43. You can find several accounts of this famous prayer meeting online, but if you'd like a more thorough account of the details and effects of the Haystack Prayer Meeting, check out *The Haystack Prayer Meeting: A Brief Account of Its Origin and Spirit* by Thomas Cole Richards (Kessinger Publishing: 2010).

44. Learn more about Lanphier and the "Layman's Prayer Revival" at https://churchleaders.com/youth/youth-leaders-blogs/148892-the-power-of-prayer.html.

45. For more on the North Korean Revival, visit https://www.thegospelcoalition.org/blogs/evangelical-history/the-north-korean-revival-of-1907/ and https://romans1015.com/1907-pyongyang-revival/.

46. www.pray.nyc.

47. Psalm 34:15; 1 Peter 3:12.

48. Walter Wink, *The Powers That Be: Theology for a New Millennium* (New York: Doubleday, 1999) 185–86.

49. Consuming Fire" by Tim Hughes (Thankyou Music: 2002).

ABOUT THE AUTHORS

JOSH HARRISON lives in Costa Mesa, California with his wife, Heather, and their three kids, Buzè, Marta, and Elijah. He serves as the pastor of Canopy Church (also in Costa Mesa) and in his free time enjoys reading, watching/coaching/playing sports, and BBQing.

TODD PROCTOR serves on the executive leadership team of Alpha USA. He partners with pastors across the nation in exploring the Alpha course, which helps churches create space for questions, hurt, and hostility toward faith in an increasingly post-Christian world. He was a founder and longtime lead pastor of Rock Harbor Church in Costa Mesa, California, leading through a season of multiplication that birthed new campuses and church plants across Orange County. Todd shares the adventure of life, ministry, and four kids with his college sweetheart and bride of three decades, Lisa.

Made in USA - Kendallville, IN
33064_9781624240638
06.25.2022 1308